CHEESE IT!

START MAKING CHEESE AT HOME TODAY

BY COLE DAWSON

Hobby Farm Press®

An Imprint of BowTie Press®

A Division of BowTie, Inc.

Irvine, California

Lead Editor: Jennifer Calvert
Art Director: Jerome Callens
Book Project Specialist: Karen Julian
Production Supervisor: Jessica Jaensch
Assistant Production Manager: Tracy Vogtman
Indexer: Melody Englund

Vice President, Chief Content Officer: June Kikuchi
Vice President, Kennel Club Books: Andrew DePrisco
BowTie Press: Jennifer Calvert, Amy Deputato, Karen Julian, Jarelle S. Stein

Text Copyright© 2012 by BowTie Press®

Front Cover Photography: Indigo Fish/Shutterstock
Back Cover Photography: Monkey Business Images/Shutterstock

All rights reserved. No part of this book may be reproduced, stored in a retrieval system, or transmitted in any form or by any means, electronic, mechanical, photocopying, recording, or otherwise, without the prior written permission of BowTie Press®, except for the inclusion of brief quotations in an acknowledged review.

Library of Congress Cataloging-in-Publication Data

Dawson, Cole, 1954-
  Cheese it! start making cheese at home today / Cole Dawson.
     p. cm.
  Includes index.
   ISBN 978-1-935484-30-1 (pbk.)
  1. Cheesemaking. 2. Cheese products. I. Title.
  SF271.D257 2012
  637'.3--dc23
                        2011048539

BowTie Press®
A Division of BowTie, Inc.
3 Burroughs
Irvine, California 92618

Printed and bound in China
18 17 16 15 14 13 12 1 2 3 4 5 6 7 8 9 10

Dedication

To the next generation of cheese makers,
whose ingenuity and hard work preserve a noble tradition.

Acknowledgments

I owe a debt of thanks to the cheese makers, food scientists, farmers, retailers, and others mentioned in this book who stole time from demanding schedules to answer my questions, show me their farms and work areas, and discuss their products. Watching a cheese maker pouring, stirring, cutting, draining, milling, and pressing day after day makes my job pecking at a computer keyboard seem like sloth. But many of today's commercial cheese makers started by experimenting in kitchens just like ours. Their efforts to bring us the tastiest American cheese—from field to table—deserve our praise and support.

I'm especially grateful to Rebecca Sherman Orozco at the American Cheese Society; cheese buyer Steve Jenkins; agricultural economist Don Blayney; food scientists Robert Ralyea, Neville McNaughton, and Paul Kindstedt; and cheese makers Rory Chase, Peter Destler, Colin McGrath, Sue Conley, Allison Hooper, Sadie Kendall, and Paula Lambert. Peter Dixon's Vermont workshops in artisan cheese making—from sourcing milk to affinage—gave me a taste of dairy magic I've tried to recreate ever since.

Homage à Fromage

Gorgonzola and sliced pears
salad sprinkled with Greek feta
give me brie with my Champagne
make me burgers topped with Cheddar.

Figs and goat cheese as a snack
apricots and Camembert
Peccorino and chianti
onion soup topped with Gruyère.

Muenster served with caraway
honey dripped on Reblochon
Asiago paired with mango
Derby cheese with Chenin Blanc.

Cow or sheep or goat's great gift
glorious cheese, to thee I sing
my love, my passion, my addiction
I crave you with everything.

—Marge Hauser

Contents

> **"Blessed are the cheese makers."**
> *—Monty Python*

Rogue Creamery's award-winning blue cheese is literally the crème de la crème.

Introduction: A New American Revolution

We all know American cheese—it tastes best melted on a burger. Commercial cream cheese spreads like chewing gum and tears our bread. Velveeta and Cheez Whiz are memorable for their eye-catching packaging and orange-yellow color, not for their flavor. Processed cheeses defined the American dairy case for decades. Until 2003.

Actually, the revolution in cheese crafting began with experiments by California goat farmers in the 1980s, but in 2003 Rogue Creamery of Oregon stole the honors at the World Cheese Awards in London with its Rogue River Blue. That's London—home to Stilton and English Cheddar. It was the beginning of a burgeoning respect for America's artisan cheese makers. In 2007, Rogue's award winner became the first raw-milk dairy product approved for export.

Liz Thorpe has tasted hundreds of fledgling *fromages* in her capacity as vice president of Murray's Cheese in Greenwich Village, New York. Says Thorpe, "As American cheeses have gotten exponentially better…it has become harder and harder to pick which to buy [for our store]. The major criterion used to be 'Is it edible?'" Now, an American cheese needs to be superlative to meet her criteria.

Cheese revolutionaries followed a path similar to California winemakers in the 1970s: they transplanted old-world traditions to their native soils, microclimates, and growing seasons. Small-scale cheese makers are now spinning milk into gold all across the country. About 500 members are registered with the American Cheese Society, whose total membership has almost tripled in the last decade. Many more hobby farmers who are not members of the association are handcrafting cheeses.

As membership has risen, so has competition for the American Cheese Society's blue ribbons. Each August, the association awards creameries for that year's best-tasting cheeses. Three states usually dominate the winner's circle—Wisconsin, Vermont, and California. In recent years, the winner's circle included Colorado, Maine, Utah, and Texas.

RIDE 'EM COWGIRLS

The story of Cowgirl Creamery offers a glimpse into the demand for handcrafted cheeses. In 1997, Sue Conley and Peggy Smith—the "cowgirls" and former chefs—started making soft cheeses using organic whole milk from a neighboring dairy in Point Reyes Station, a hamlet north of San Francisco. Today, the company comprises two creameries (at Point Reyes and Petaluma), three stores, and a mail-order business. From a single recipe for their award-winning Mt. Tam, the creamery now offers ten varieties, producing about 3,000 pounds of cheese a week.

"We were lucky," says Peggy Smith. "Right about the time we opened Cowgirl Creamery, people were ready to expand their knowledge and their appetite for cheese. They had explored the word of wine, they'd learned about vinegars, they were using Italian olive oils and demanding good, crusty breads. Cheese was just waiting to be discovered."

From the start, Cowgirl Creamery's handcrafted cheeses benefitted from local organic whole milk.

A true appreciation for cheese begins with the first taste of a carefully crafted artisan variety.

Americans' expanding appetite for cheese created a desire for variety when eating out as well as eating in. Selling directly to restaurants is a lucrative business for farmers. Laura Chenel, a goat-cheese pioneer, got her start in 1979 when Alice Waters of Chez Panisse put Chenel's chèvre on the menu. The cheese plate is nearly ubiquitous in fine restaurants today, and that trend has sent sales soaring.

When master cheesemonger (the manager of a specialty cheese department or shop) Steven Jenkins wrote his classic *The Cheese Primer* in 1996, he recommended thirty "best American cheeses" to readers. Today, that list would be a book in itself. "North American artisanal cheeses," he says, "have reached a level that puts them on par with the artisanal cheeses of Europe, both in quality and variety." Jenkins should know; in 1980, he became the first American "Cheese Knight," or Chevalier du Taste-Fromage.

SAY CHEESE

If so much exciting cheese is readily available, why bother to make it at home? Three reasons: health (yours, the animals', and the environment's), savings, and satisfaction. With a small investment of money and time, novice cheese makers can make perfect soft cheeses that can be eaten right away, including ricotta, paneer, mozzarella, mascarpone, and cottage cheese. With a bit more investment in ingredients, supplies, and time, they can make semi-hard cheeses such as Colby, Jack, and Cheddar. After tasting success, a serious artisan may move on to tackle mold- and bacteria-ripened cheeses such as Camembert, Stilton, Gorgonzola, and Muenster.

Redwood Hill's Sharon Bice helps create the creamery's signature chèvre.

Need more inspiration? Seek out family-run creameries in your area. If they offer tours, you'll see the miraculous alchemy of cheese-in-the-making—a blend of art and science. Many creameries are closed to the public for logistical reasons (small operations would be overwhelmed by visitors) or hygienic reasons (cheese making demands a strictly controlled environment). But others welcome visitors, who can roam the grounds, pet the herds, meet the cheese makers, sample the product line, and ask questions.

Successful cheese making takes practice (what doesn't?), but by trial and error, you'll understand more about dairy foods than you ever would simply by buying them ready-made on supermarket shelves. Homemade also tastes better, and you can tweak the recipe any way you want to.

WHAT ABOUT THAT FANCY WORD, *ARTISANAL*?

An artisan is a craftsperson whose products are made by hand. The American Cheese Society defines artisanal cheese as "a cheese produced primarily by hand, in small batches, with particular attention paid to the tradition of the cheese-maker's art, and thus using as little mechanization as possible in the production of cheese. Artisan, or artisanal, cheeses may be made from all types of milk and may include various flavorings."

Cowgirl Creamery marries commercial efficiency with personal involvement to create their artisan cheeses.

To classify as *farmstead*, a cheese must be made using milk from the farmer's own herd or flock on the farm where the animals are raised. Milk used in the production of farmstead cheeses may not be obtained from any outside source. Farmstead cheeses may also be made from all types of milk and may include various flavorings. So all farmstead cheese is artisanal, but not all artisanal cheese is farmstead.

A simpler way to define artisanal cheese making is "getting your hands in the curds." This book is designed to help you get your hands in the curds. If you follow directions carefully, especially the cleanliness tips, we can almost guarantee that you'll be on your way to a culinary adventure that is whey cool. But first, a bit of history.

Paula Lambert of the Mozzarella Company rolls up her sleeves for the cheese-making process.

WHAT'S IN A NAME?

Most cheese names reflect their origins as the product of a regional artisan. Emmental is a valley in Switzerland, Brie de Meaux is a town near Paris, Cotswold comes from the Cotswolds region of England, and Roquefort translates as "strong rock," a reference to the limestone caves where it is still aged. Other names denote some unique quality. Raclette, from the French *racler*, means "to scrape," which is how this melted cheese is served; Reblochon is from the French *reblocher*, which means "to milk again"; ricotta, "recooked" in Italian, is made from leftover whey. And still others refer to both region and a distinguishing feature. Monterey Jack, for example, refers both to the Monterey region of California and a cheese press called a "house jack," which was brought to California from Spain by eighteenth-century Franciscan monks.

Cotswold cheese is as uniquely lovely as the region for which it was named.

THE WORD ON CURDS

As a cheese maker, you'll be practicing an art that's as old as the pyramids—and tastier. Archeological digs in Egypt unearthed cheese-making pots and cheese remnants in the tomb of Horus-Aha (circa 3000 BC). In southern Iraq, scientists found a Sumerian frieze of priests milking their animals and curdling their milk. Sumerians were the first to practice intensive year-round agriculture (from about 5300 BC), including making cheese.

At its simplest, cheese is a way to preserve milk, a precious commodity. Cheese is a reliable protein source available in any season, which is why the very early British called it "white meat." They figured out that it was more economical to get protein from milk and its by-products than to kill their animals for red meat and have to replace them. The rich usually ate both meat and soft (fresh) cheese, while the poor ate no meat and only hard cheese. This was the birth of the expression *hard cheese*, meaning "bad luck."

Cheese was so crucial to the ancient Romans that the Emperor Diocletian (284 to 305 AD) set a maximum price for it, trying to meet demand by limiting cost. Columella, in *De Re Rustica* (1 AD), the most complete and informative guide to Roman agriculture, tells us that Romans preferred

Several French cheeses have their roots in the rich history of the country's abbeys.

their curd cheeses smoked, salted, and flavored with herbs and spices. Cato, Horace, and Apicius, all influential writers of the time, wrote about their favorite cheese dishes. And we know that Romans introduced those dishes—along with aqueducts, amphitheaters, and paved roads—to the lands they conquered.

Enter the barbarians—the Visigoths, Vandals, and Huns—who were not cheese eaters. Is it any wonder that this historical period is referred to as the Dark Ages? At monasteries during this time, the secrets of beer, wine, and cheese fermentation were carefully guarded and refined. Cheeses originally made by monks and nuns during this time retain their original names today—Port du Salut from the Monastery of Notre Dame du Port Salut in Laval, France; Maroilles from the Abbey of Maroilles in Avesnes, France; and Wenslydale from an abbey in Yorkshire, England.

Legend has it that Abbé Charles-Jean Bonvoust, a priest seeking refuge during the French Revolution, taught the recipe for Camembert to a Norman farmer's wife, Marie Harel, who housed him. True or not, we can assume thousands of farm wives throughout Europe passed "secret" recipes on to their children. Europe's Industrial Revolution changed this tradition, as it did nearly every aspect of the rural economy. Soon farmers were bringing their milk to cheese-making factories, or creameries, the first of which opened in Bern, Switzerland, in 1815. Cheese was cooked in copper kettles over fire pits; rennet (used to coagulate milk) was made from the stomach lining of a calf. By 1900, Europe boasted 750 cheese factories.

Upstart Americans weren't far behind. In 1851, a dairy farmer named Jesse Williams founded the first cheese factory in Rome, New York, producing four Cheddar cheeses a day, each weighing at least 150 pounds. Cheddar remains popular with Americans, who, prior to the twenty-first century, consumed and produced more of it than any other variety. (Mozzarella overtook Cheddar in 2003 to become America's most popular cheese, thanks mainly to pizza.) While the British brought Cheddar to New England, other New World immigrants—German, Swiss, Italian—brought over their own cheese-making traditions and planted them where they settled.

America excelled in the mass production of cheese. Jesse Williams and other nineteenth-century manufacturers developed the scientific methods and assembly-line processes used in commercial cheese making. Today, modern cheese-processing plants run hygienically and efficiently. Steam-jacketed, stainless-steel vats have replaced wood-fired copper kettles; refrigeration has replaced caves; rotary knives cut curds; and computers monitor temperature and acidity.

Automation swept aside the art of farmstead cheese making with, some say, a predictable loss of quality and regional variation. But for the cheese-making hobbyist, centuries-old methods have changed little. We still seek out milk from grass-fed animals, cut the curds, drain the whey, and press our precious rounds by hand. Rediscovering the lost art of cheese making is practical as well as satisfying. It teaches us about the food we eat and increases our self-sufficiency and independence in a world of mass production and consumerism.

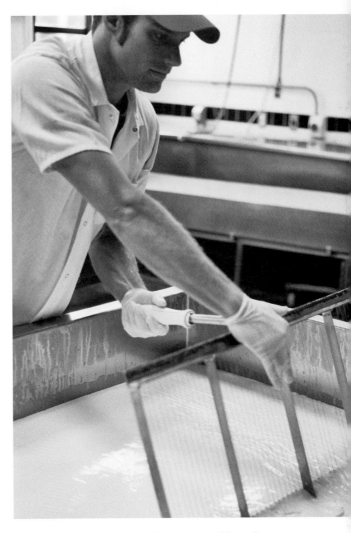

While creameries produce larger quantities of cheese than you will at home, their methods are roughly the same as yours will be.

Creamy Camembert is just one of the delicious cheeses you can make for yourself and others.

TYPES OF CHEESE

As we have discussed, cheese originated as a way to preserve milk without refrigeration. But terrain, climate, and resources limited cheese makers. Paul Kindstedt, a professor in the department of Nutrition and Food Sciences at the University of Vermont and co-director of the Vermont Institute for Artisan Cheese, says, "Cheese makers had to do things differently from one region to the next because of different constraints." He reduces about 1,400 cheese varieties to just twenty families, such as Alpine cheese, soft-ripened cheese, and so on. In his book *American Farmstead Cheese* (2005), Kindstedt defines *family* as "a group of cheeses that share a similar manufacturing technology and possess a similar initial chemical composition."

"Whatever cheese you favor," says Kindstedt, "there's a good reason it arose in history when it did and where it did." In the Swiss Alps and eastern France, for example, where Emmental, Gruyère, and Beaufort originated, farmers needed large, durable cheeses for the long, arduous trip to market in the lower valleys. That meant they needed cheese with low moisture. The cardinal rule of cheese: the higher the moisture content, the shorter the shelf life.

In contrast to Alpine cheeses, soft-ripened cheeses such as Camembert and Brie reflect the practical needs of farm wives for a cheese that was easy to make and small enough to consume at home or sell at market. Their product didn't need to withstand the rigors of transport and long storage time, so it didn't need to be low in moisture content, cooked at high temperatures, or pressed with weights.

Like farm wives, monks in Europe's abbeys invented cheeses suited to their needs using simple workable methods. Camembert and Muenster are both soft-ripened cheeses with similar moisture content. But the difference in taste and texture, Kindstedt explains, is because these two groups of cheese makers—farm wives and monks—differed in the time they allowed to elapse between milking and making their cheeses. One suited the monastic schedule, the other the farm wives' schedule. These two types of soft-ripened cheese are called *washed-rind* and *bloomy-rind.*

A BETTER WHEY

Making our own cheese allows us to travel across geography and time to meet those Franciscan friars or Italian shepherds or Greek housewives, to learn their kitchen rituals, and to recreate and perhaps improve upon their recipes. We can be as inventive as they once were. We can have our cheese and eat it, too.

As consumers, we want to know where our food comes from, and many of us are taking steps to live and farm sustainably. Unlike thirty years ago when American cheese makers were pioneering, it's not hard to find resources to help you in your efforts. Using this book, you can short-circuit the commodity pipeline and take charge of your family's care and feeding. You'll learn that:

✤ Homemade cheese is fresher, healthier, and tastier than processed cheese.

✤ You have control over the end product and can tweak your recipe any way you want.

✤ Making cheese at home is cost effective: after buying some simple equipment, you'll save money.

✤ If you're buying local milk and/or selling your product, you're contributing to your local economy.

✤ Making your own cheese reduces strain on the planet's natural resources.

✤ It's creative and fun, and you can count on impressing family and friends with your homemade gifts.

Once you've tasted cheese lovingly prepared with your own hands, you'll never look back.

CHAPTER 1

Old-World Style, New-World Flavor

When my grandparents were growing up in upstate New York a century ago, dairy farmers sent their milk to local cheese factories. These dairy "factories" were often cooperatives that were member-owned and -operated. Their names still stand—Creamery Lane or Cheese Hill—even if they are long gone. During long winters, when the herd's milk supply dwindled, creamery cheese generated much-needed income.

As family farms disappeared across the landscape, consolidation became an economic necessity. Vermont's Cabot Creamery is a prime example. In 1919, ninety-four Vermont farmers pooled their resources and paid five dollars per cow. Today, Cabot has 1,274 member farms in New England and upstate New York and sells a ton of its prize-winning Cheddar. Foremost Farms, headquartered in Wisconsin, draws milk from 2,300 members; Land O' Lakes draws from 7,000 farmers and 1,300 local cooperatives in 50 states.

However, these cheese factories are not "cheddaring" by hand, the old-fashioned way. In contrast to the artisanal

> "Twenty years ago, if it wasn't French or Italian, it wasn't cheese. It wasn't edible."
>
> —Allison Hooper, Vermont Butter and Cheese Company

process, called *open-vat cheese making*, commercial cheese plants rely on automation. From the time milk enters the plant until the finished cheese is packaged, it never touches human hands. Factories produce for volume and consistency. Like anything else mass-produced, commodity cheese relies on computer technology to ensure that the product never varies, that it meets production quotas, and that it is heat treated. (Sanitation has changed dramatically since my grandparents bought cheese. Farmers no longer bring their milk to factories in oak barrels. Today, milk is shipped from farms in closed containers and refrigerated.) Thankfully, a few brave dairy farmers and cheese makers have jumped the assembly line.

In the next chapter, we will look at how large-scale dairy farming affected the herds being bred for commercial milk. Suffice it to say that, in the switch from farm to factory, milk drinkers lost taste, quality, and a quirkiness that distinguish regional cheese making. Small-scale cheese makers know that, as the seasons and grazing conditions change, so, too, does the cheese. What Kraft might see as a flaw, the artisan sees as a source of pride.

The goal of large commercial dairies is to produce as much cheese as inexpensively as possible. The goal of small creameries and home cheese makers? Simply to make the best cheese.

ARTISAN VERSUS COMMODITY CHEESE

The main difference between artisan and commodity cheese makers is their treatment of milk and the animals that produce it. Artisans favor grass-fed animals because they create richer, more flavorful milk. Industry giants use feed and antibiotics to boost production and keep herds healthy, often with results that are unhealthy for consumers.

Another difference is that artisans modify their recipes to accommodate changes in milk while industries modify the milk. Cheese manufacturers change the animals' feed, grazing conditions, lactation, and so on to get a more consistent raw product. For artisans, the food source can't be denaturalized without affecting the quality of the end product—the cheese.

While uniformity may be necessary for grocery-store shelves, an artisan appreciates slight imperfections in his cheese.

RESPECT THE COWS

Reasons other than an avoidance of size and mechanization motivate today's cheese crafters. One is their respect for ecology and the local economy. At Jasper Hill Farm in Vermont's Northeast Kingdom, Andy and Mateo Kehler and their wives Victoria and Angie view cheese making as a return to family farming that's deeply rooted in the Green Mountain State.

"We started Jasper Hill Farm in the summer of 1998," explains Mateo. "Greensboro lost five dairy farms that year, a blow to the working landscape that beautifies this part of the world. In July 2002, we purchased fifteen Ayrshire heifers, and so began our adventure in sustainable agricultural development." The Kehlers' approach to dairying supports Vermont's push to increase agritourism as a way of boosting the local economy. Any tourist who's followed the Vermont Cheese Trail admires the state's commitment to farmers like the Kehlers.

Manufacturers see the dairying process differently. Milk is perishable, and to extend its shelf life, it must be manipulated until it bears no resemblance to what comes out of a cow, goat, or sheep. Mega-dairies pack cows into huge cement lots, where they are milked several times a day. This shortens the cows' lives (though it may boost company profits). Healthy cows live from thirteen to fifteen years; cows bred for industry are sent to slaughter when they are "spent," sometimes after only three years.

A CRAFTY BUSINESS

Another word for artisan is craft. Let's define *craft* as a trade or occupation requiring manual skill. Modern cheese making involves a lot of machines. Curd cutting, vat storing, measuring acidity levels and coagulation, and wheel pressing are all automated. But a true cheesewright will tell you that a machine cannot make decisions about milk's taste, smell, texture, and consistency as it is turned into cheese. In general, artisan cheese makers favor:

❖ handcrafting over mechanization,

❖ fresh over shelf-stable,

❖ local milk over milk that's shipped long distances,

❖ clean—but not sterile—milk with a balance of natural bacteria,

❖ milk without artificial growth hormones,

❖ milk from animals that eat what they are biologically designed to eat, and

❖ milk from animals that are clean and healthy.

Look for locally made cheese in specialty cheese shops and at farmers' markets.

NEW BREEDS OF CHEESE

It isn't surprising that when new American cheese makers started experimenting in the early 1980s, they defined themselves as the opposite of industrial cheese makers. At the time, cheese was synonymous with cow's milk, so they started breeding goats for milk and cheese. Asked about her reasons for starting to breed Alpine goats, Mary Keehn of Cypress Grove in Arcata, California, explains that her four children were allergic to cow's milk. She began, as so many farmers do, to make cheese from a surplus of milk and to sell it to raise money.

Let's recall that in 1983, when Keehn was trying to sell to local markets, she was competing with foreign imports. No one was whipping up batches of goat cheese except a few enterprising women like her. The first of these to successfully sell and market her fresh chèvre (goat's milk cheese) was Laura Chenel in 1979 in Sebastopol, California. Chenel studied in France with the master of goat-cheese production, Jean-Claude Le Jaouen, before experimenting in her own kitchen.

Chenel's neighbors at the time were Jennifer Bice and Steve Schack, who owned Redwood Hill Farm. They were also promoting the health benefits of goat's milk, and because Sonoma County had birthed the Back to the Land movement, there was a thirst for raw milk products among the hippie crowd. Not everyone was so enthusiastic. "In those days," says Bice, "we didn't even tell people what they were eating because they had too many preconceptions." Forty years later, Redwood's products have grown BC (beyond chèvre) to feta and aged cheeses such as Bucheret, Camellia, and Crottin.

If you want the best cheese, you should start with farm-fresh milk.

The delight of sweet-tasting goat cheese was a catalyst for Allison Hooper to found Vermont Butter and Cheese Company in 1983 with her business partner Bob Reese. "When I worked on a farm in Brittany, France," she remembers, "I was surprised to discover I loved the taste of goat's milk cheese. It wasn't bucky or rancid. If the goats are clean, well cared for, and you separate the bucks from the does, the result is a mild, not a strong, flavor."

Not all milk comes from cows: some of the most flavorful cheese is made from the milk of goats, sheep, and even water buffalo.

But My Doctor Says...

If you are on a low-cholesterol, low-sodium, or low-fat diet, you can still eat cheese—in small portions. Those small portions pack a lot of nutrition. Your doctor will agree that unprocessed cheese is an excellent source of calcium, protein, and phosphorus. Though cheese is high in saturated fat, a healthy diet allows this to account for up to 10 percent of total daily fat intake. Those on a low-sodium diet should stick to fresh, unsalted cheeses, such as chèvre, not cheese that requires salt as a preservative, flavor enhancer, or dehydrator, such as feta. Good things—like real cheese—come in small packages.

Soon Hooper was taking her own versions of chèvre and crème fraîche on the road. But the challenge for these American pioneers was getting restaurants and retailers to try their new products. Chenel connected with chef Alice Waters at Chez Panisse in San Francisco; Hooper sold to chefs in New York and Boston.

These new cheeses were not for melting, grating, or stuffing into a sandwich; they were for eating. They tasted uniquely delicious. But in the 1980s, few Americans wanted cheese from a goat. In 1990, a second wave of new American cheese makers—David and Cindy Majors at Vermont Shepherd and Tom and Nancy Clark at Old Chatham Sheepherding Company in New York—started making sheep's milk cheese. But it wasn't until 2000 that a healthy market for specialty cheese emerged.

Sadie Kendall of Kendall Farms wanted to be a lawyer. She invented a crème fraîche that chefs love because it stabilizes and lightens their French sauces. This talent might be genetic. "My grandmother's name was Cloutier, and her roots: Normandy," admits Kendall. She, too, started making goat cheese in California in the early 1980s, and soon connected with local chef Ian McPhee. "I would take my experimental batches of crème fraîche to Ian in San Luis Obispo, and he would test them, boil them, beat them." The result was a crème fraîche more heat-stable than either the French version or sour cream—a product specifically created for the best chefs in the country.

Paula Lambert was inspired by her post-college years in Italy to try to duplicate the mozzarella she had enjoyed there. "When I first traveled to Italy in the early 1960s and tasted fresh mozzarella, I couldn't quite decide what I was eating. It was so soft and moist, very bland and milky tasting, almost spongy, and oozing with milk. Later, I learned that some of this fresh mozzarella was made from the milk of water buffalo and some from cow's milk. I loved the fresh mozzarella in Italy, and because it wasn't available in Dallas, I founded the Mozzarella Company in 1982."

Tom and Nancy Clark bought 600 acres and 115 sheep in 1993 to launch the Old Chatham Sheepherding Company. Their flock of East Frisian crossbred sheep is now over 1,000 strong, making it the largest sheep dairy in the United States. Old Chatham is famous for its Hudson Valley Camembert, a mix of sheep's and cow's milk; Ewe's Blue; and a line of sheep's milk yogurts.

Though Chenel sold her business to the French conglomerate Rians Group in 2006, we still enjoy our goat cheese salads thanks, in part, to her. Today, about 500 registered cheese makers are making milk from goats, cows, and sheep in all fifty states. Their recipe for success: make good cheese, learn how to promote it, and find ways to sell it.

A SENSE OF PLACE

With a resurgence of farmstead cheese making, American artisans embrace the concept of *terroir* as well as its European roots. They borrow the French term from winemakers. *Terroir* means "sense of place," all those subtle local influences that determine a cheese's flavor and texture, such as terrain, vegetation, climate, subsoil, breed of animal, and season. Dairy scientist and co-director of the Vermont Institute for Artisan Cheese Paul Kindstedt explains that, as standardization came to dominate the cheese industry after 1851, farmstead cheese making all but disappeared—and with it, the reverence for *terroir*. "The science of cheese making," he writes in *American Farmstead Cheese*, "triumphed over the art of cheese making." Regional cheeses on the market today—Humboldt Fog, Georgia Pecan, Oregonzola—revel in their agricultural landscapes.

Artisan cheese makers agree that what creates demand for their products is flavor, and the richest, most flavorful milk comes from pasture-fed animals. First, it's healthier for the animals than feeding them silage indoors. Second, it's healthier for those of us who consume their milk as cheese. Grazing cows, for example, eat grass and return its nutritional value to the land as cow patties, which makes more sense than expending energy hauling feed into and manure out of the barn. Better to put that energy into creating the most efficient small farm you can.

Whether it's Italian mozzarella or French Brie, the cheese you love is often reminiscent of the places you love.

CHAPTER 2

Milk Basics

If you've ever left a glass of milk on a warm stove overnight, you know that *curdling* (acidification) is a natural process. As a cheese maker, you'll be working with nature and helping it along by adding bacteria and enzymes, which is why it's important to begin with the freshest, least-altered milk.

First, let's put milk under the microscope. It's often called "nature's perfect food" for a reason: it supplies almost all of the nutrients and vitamins our bodies require. Milk's main ingredients are water, fat, casein, whey protein, and lactose.

♣ Water holds proteins in suspension and comprises 80 to 87 percent of milk, depending on the animal.

♣ Fat plays a key role in aroma, flavor, and texture. Ripened cheeses such as Camembert and Muenster have creamy textures and melt-in-your-mouth flavor because of high butterfat content.

♣ Casein is milk's major protein. Because of its unique chemical structure, it can be made to shrink or expand, giving cheeses like mozzarella elasticity.

> "Behind every piece of cheese lies a little bit of earth and sky."
> —*Italo Calvino, novelist*

♣ Whey is a by-product of making cheese and can be used to make other cheeses such as ricotta and gjetost. Whey protein comprises only 0.6 percent of milk. It is soluble in milk, retains more moisture than casein, and is nonelastic.

♣ Lactose is milk sugar and the engine that starts the fermentation process. Without lactose, there's no cheese.

A DIFFERENT ANIMAL ALTOGETHER

All milk contains those five elements, but there are differences in breeds of cow, goat, and sheep that have a marked effect on cheese making. Use the table "Average Composition of Milk and Cheese Yield" to see the differences.

AVERAGE COMPOSITION OF MILK AND CHEESE YIELD

ANIMAL	% FAT	% PROTEIN	% LACTOSE	% TOTAL SOLIDS	% YIELD
Cow	3.7	3.4	4.8	12.7	Fresh: 20–25 Semi-Hard: 12–15 Hard: 10–12
Goat	3.6	3.5	4.5	12.4	Fresh: 18–20 Semi-Hard: 10–12 Hard: 8–10
Sheep	7.4	4.5	4.8	19.3	Fresh: 30–50 Semi-Hard: 20–25 Hard: 15–20

COW'S MILK

One of the dairy farms I remember from when I was growing up was called Brown Swiss. That's a type of cow once popular, as was the Jersey, for its high butterfat content. How high? A Jersey's milk can be as high as 5.4 percent fat, Brown Swiss up to 4.5 percent. Holsteins, preferred by commercial dairies, provide milk with 3 to 4 percent fat. But Holsteins, unlike Brown Swiss or Jerseys, can yield up to 10 gallons of milk a day (holy cow!). Not surprisingly, Holsteins now make up 90 percent of our dairy cow population of 9 million.

Cows and bulls were among the first immigrants to arrive in Jamestown in 1607. It was the beginning of dairying in America—and the beginning of some prosperity for colonists. Dairy cattle like open spaces, abundant vegetation, and temperate climates, so they adapted well to their new home, giving milk that was rich with high moisture content and large fat globules that rose to the surface as cream—in other words, this milk was ideal for cheese making.

On the farm, milking occurred twice a day, and cheeses were a mixture of the morning milk and that of the previous evening. Today's commercial cows are bred to produce huge quantities of milk—three times as much as the old-fashioned cow—and are given special feed and antibiotics. Their milk may contain high levels of artificial growth hormone from their pituitary glands. A 2007 US Department of Agriculture (USDA) dairy survey estimated 15.2 percent of dairies used

These Holstein cows are the breed preferred by dairies for their tremendous milk output.

rBGH (artificial growth hormones approved by the FDA for use in commercial dairies) on 17.2 percent of cows.

Regional creameries such as Cowgirl and Rogue are encouraging American dairy farmers to bring back a wider variety of herds. European dairy farmers are still raising cows more for butter, yogurt, and cheese than for bulk fluid milk—that is to say, for quality rather than quantity. These traditional herds include the red cow of Italy's Parmigiano-Reggiano region and the Innisfail Shorthorn, used to make English Cheddar.

GOAT'S MILK

Unlike milk cows, goats can survive extreme climates with poor vegetation and—as everyone knows—aren't picky about what they eat. Goat's milk is partly homogenized and has smaller fat globules than cow's milk, yielding cheese with smooth consistency and tangy flavor. Though goats in the United States have only been raised for cheese making in the past twenty-five years, it's common practice elsewhere in the world.

Goats produce more milk than sheep do—about 1 gallon a day—and lactate for about ten months (the same as cows). But because they yield much less than cows, their milk tends to be consumed quickly. Fresh goat's milk cheese is snowy white because its yellow beta-carotene has been converted to colorless vitamin A. Spring and summer cheeses made with goat's milk have the full grassy flavor of pasture-fed animals. Of the major breeds of US dairy goats—Alpine, LaMancha, Nubian, Saanen, Oberhasli, and Toggenburg—Nubians boast the highest butterfat and milk solids. Saanens give the most milk and are known as the Holsteins of dairy goats.

Goat's milk might be a bit harder to come by, but check your area for farms and your supermarket for specialty dairy sections.

Sheep's milk may be rare, but it's worth hunting around for.

SHEEP'S MILK

Sheep, with their wooly coats, can survive harsh climates in areas with little water or vegetation—places like Mongolia, Australia, and the mountains of Greece and Sicily. Fully homogenized, sheep's milk is denser than either cow's or goat's milk. A cow might produce 7 gallons a day to a sheep's 2 quarts, but the amount of solids is about the same. Unfortunately, the dairy-sheep industry is just getting started in America, so sheep's milk is like gold—and priced accordingly. East Frisian sheep are the best producers; if you can find some, you're in luck.

Tom and Nancy Clark did just that in 1994 when they started Old Chatham Sheepherding Company in upstate New York with 150 East Frisian crossbreds. Cindy and David Majors of Vermont Shepherd also pioneered sheep dairying in the Northeast. When they decided to get serious about making cheese from their flock of East Frisians, they went to the French Pyrenees to learn from Basques, who had perfected their techniques for centuries.

FORMS OF MILK

Many hobby farmers start making cheese because their milk animals give them more milk than they can drink. Other cheese makers want the cheese without the work of caring for and feeding animals. In that case, they buy milk from local dairies. No local dairies? Grocery store milk is OK as long as you know what to avoid.

Locating fresh milk can be challenging. Why? Because what's most convenient to purchase—ultra-pasteurized milk—will not make great cheese. First, let's define the process called *pasteurization*.

In 1857, the French chemist and microbiologist Louis Pasteur discovered that heat treatment would remove unwanted microbes—this process is named after him. Soon, both Europe and America adopted pasteurization of food and beverages to ensure consumer safety. Dairy herds increased, milk was shipped cross-country, and milk and cheese plants stored milk longer. By 1940, the pasteurization process was well established.

The USDA requires milk to be heated to 161 degrees Fahrenheit for fifteen seconds to qualify for the "pasteurized" label. This process is called *High Temperature Short Time* (HTST). Also acceptable is heating milk to 145 degrees Fahrenheit for thirty minutes, which is called *Low Temperature Long Time* (LTLT) or *vat pasteurization*.

Ultra-pasteurization (UP) uses a range of milk-processing temperatures from 191 to 212 degrees Fahrenheit for varying times. All milk fitting this definition must be labeled "ultra-pasteurized." Heating milk above 174 degrees Fahrenheit destabilizes whey proteins and prevents a good curd, so avoid a UP label if you're making cheese from store-bought milk. Along the same lines is *Ultra Heat Treatment* (UHT), which is used for milk that's sold in boxes and doesn't need refrigeration until opened. UHT heats milk at a whopping 275 to 300 degrees Fahrenheit. Both UP and UHT processes wipe out friendly bacteria and are unsuitable for making cheese.

Why, you might ask, would dairies sterilize their milk in the first place? For one thing, it extends milk's shelf life from eighteen to sixty days. For another, unhealthy cows carry diseases. Dairies turn the heat up under their vats in the hope of destroying these pathogens—often without success. Proper herd management is the better solution.

Look for the UP label. Ultra-pasteurized milk is unsuitable for making cheese.

RAW MILK

Raw milk comes straight from the animal, and the most desirable raw milk—because it benefits the animals' health and natural habitat—comes from grass-fed herds. For cheese makers, raw milk has a complexity and depth of flavor that pasteurized milk can never match. "Pasteurization removes all of nature's programming in the milk," says Neville McNaughton, a St. Louis-based dairy technologist. "It kills the flavor-producing enzymes, which the cheese maker then has to add back in, putting the cheese back into the cheese."

Many European cheeses are made using raw, unpasteurized milk for this reason, but you won't find them in your grocery store's dairy case. The USDA requires that any raw-milk cheese sold be aged at least sixty days at temperatures above 34 degrees Fahrenheit. That eliminates the best brands of Camembert, for example. But hobby cheese makers who can get a clean source of milk should try using it unpasteurized and compare the two. Just be 100 percent sure that the milk is clean and the farm animals that produced it have been tested by a qualified veterinarian. (See "Testing Raw Milk" on page 30.)

If your state allows the purchase of raw milk, try it out in some of your cheese recipes.

The buying and selling of raw milk is strictly controlled and varies by state. As of this writing, raw milk can be legally sold in only twenty-eight states. Another option to explore is a cow-share program in which consumers pay a farmer to care for and milk their cow(s). They essentially own a share of the milk produced and don't have to purchase it.

The Weston A. Price Foundation's website www.realmilk.com/why.html lists sources of raw milk in states where it's legal to buy it. Real Milk is a campaign to encourage us to drink milk from old-fashioned breeds such as Jerseys, Guernseys, Red Devons, Brown Swiss, and older genetic lines of Holsteins; to favor grass-fed herds; and to avoid homogenized milk (to drink milk with the cream on top). More information is available at www.raw-milk-facts.com.

When making cheese using raw milk, it's important to top-stir it (stir just the top ¼ inch of the milk) so that the butterfat that's risen to the surface mixes with the rest of the milk. To sum up:

❖ Raw milk makes rich-flavored cheese but may be hard to find.

❖ Pasteurized milk is readily available, but you need to add calcium chloride during cheese making if you are using homogenized milk.

❖ Pasteurized milk has fewer enzymes than raw milk and tastes flatter.

TESTING RAW MILK

Healthy milk comes from healthy animals whose udders are free of mastitis (inflammation of the udder caused by bacterial infection). To play it safe, pasteurize your raw milk according to the directions below before making cheese. You can also invest in a California Mastitis Test (CMT) kit for cow's or goat's milk. This inexpensive kit detects high levels of somatic cells, which may indicate a mastitis infection. It's crucial for cheese makers because no one wants bitter rancid cheese.

HOW TO PASTEURIZE RAW MILK

1. Heat your milk slowly in a stainless-steel pot or double boiler to 145 degrees Fahrenheit (use a dairy thermometer). Stir gently.

2. Keep the temperature of the milk at 145 degrees Fahrenheit for exactly thirty minutes—not shorter, not longer.

3. Cool the milk to cheese-making temperature by quickly immersing the pot in a sink of ice water and stirring.

4. If you can't make cheese right away (always preferable), cool the milk to 40 degrees Fahrenheit. Store it refrigerated at that temperature for up to five days.

OTHER TYPES OF MILK

Homogenized milk. The process of breaking down fat globules in milk to smaller than 2 micrometers is called *homogenization*. At that size, the butterfat or cream doesn't rise to the surface. But curd does not coagulate as easily in milk that's been homogenized. This type of milk can be used to make cheese by adding more rennet than recipes call for as well as calcium chloride, a salt that absorbs moisture and helps curdling.

Creamline milk. This is unhomogenized milk with a line that separates the top cream from the milk at the bottom. Milk that retains its original ingredients and a butterfat content of 3.5 to 4 percent is called *whole milk*.

Nonfat (skim) milk. Milk that has a butterfat content of 1 to 2 percent is called *nonfat* or *skim milk*. Nonfat milk is used to prepare starter cultures (active lactic acid–producing bacteria that "start" the process of cheese making) and to make hard grating cheeses such as Parmesan. It can also be used as a low-fat alternative for the fresh-cheese recipes in this book. Keep in mind, though, that any cheese made with nonfat or low-fat milk will be drier and less flavorful than cheeses made with whole milk.

Dry milk powder. You can use dehydrated milk solids (especially when fresh milk isn't available) to make soft cheeses, yogurt, and other dairy products.

If you're watching your waistline, try fresh cheeses such as ricotta that are naturally low in butterfat.

A WORD ABOUT BUTTERFAT

Cheese labeling can be confusing if you're watching your fat intake. A label that reads "50 percent butterfat" doesn't mean that half the cheese is fat; it means that half the cheese solids are fat, or about 25 percent of the cheese as a whole. If you are on a reduced-fat diet, stick to cheeses naturally low in butterfat. These include fresh cheeses such as ricotta, fromage blanc, cottage cheese, and part-skim mozzarella. Some of the recipes in this book can be made using nonfat and low-fat milk, but the yield will be less than when using whole milk.

Actually, cheese is very nutritious, and our bodies know how to break it down and use it. Butterfat contains vitamins A and D, which are needed for assimilation of the calcium and protein contained in the watery part of milk (whey). Without these vitamins, protein and calcium are more difficult to use and can possibly become toxic. Butterfat is rich in short- and medium-chain fatty acids that protect against disease and stimulate the immune system. It also contains glycosphingolipids that prevent intestinal distress and conjugated linoleic acid (CLA), which has strong anticancer properties.

Freezing Your Milk

You can't freeze cow's or goat's milk without damaging it for cheese making, but you can make it into curd first and then freeze it. Cheese makers often use frozen curds during the winter when their animals are indoors. Frozen curds also work if you can't find fresh milk or if you want to supplement the milk you have. You can freeze sheep's milk in liquid form.

You are what you eat...and what they eat. Buy milk only from responsible sources.

CHANGES IN MILK CHEMISTRY

Remember the phrase "You are what you eat"? Whatever a milk animal eats affects the quality of its milk and cheese. Type of feed, season of the year, stage of lactation, and the animal's health all influence milk production. What type of vegetation does the animal graze on, for example, and how many months is it allowed outside? When animals are unable to graze and they go completely *on-feed*, as it is called, the nature of the milk changes, even when the quality of the feed—grain, hay, or fermented hay (silage)—is very high. Seasonal changes are so important to European cheese makers that some of their products are identified as "winter" and "summer."

More important to milk composition than feed or the weather, however, is the animal's lactation cycle. Dairy animals usually (but not always) give birth in springtime, and the milk created during lactation is particularly concentrated (high in butterfat and protein) to nourish the new offspring. When baby animals begin eating solid food (grazing), the butterfat in the mother's milk decreases, and the volume increases. Milk produced during the first week of lactation (called *colostrum*) is unstable, as is milk produced during late-stage lactation.

FRESH IS BEST

There's an old saying: "You can't make good cheese from bad milk." If you are not milking your own animals, buy from a local dairy. The closer your milk is to its source, the better it is for making cheese. Any of the recipes in this book will work with pasteurized or homogenized whole, skim, or low-fat store-bought milk as long as it hasn't been ultra-pasteurized (UP). Of course, cheese made using whole milk will taste better because of its higher butterfat content.

Supporting local dairies is not just a good deed—their milk is the best foundation for your cheese.

CHAPTER 3

How to Make Cheese

Whether your milk comes from a cow, goat, sheep, water buffalo, camel, or yak—and they're all used in cheese making—it contains five components: water, lactose (milk sugar), fat, protein (whey and casein), and minerals. The goal in making cheese from any type of milk is to expel water and condense the solids.

"Never cry over sour milk. Just make it into cottage cheese."

—Old saying

Each cheese will have its own water, acid, and salt content, which influence its ripening and final aroma, texture, and flavor. Cheddar cheese, for example, starts with a moisture content of 87 percent and the cheese maker must squeeze out enough water (or liquid whey) to reduce that down to 36 percent. Cottage cheese, on the other hand, retains more whey. (See the table below)

COMPOSITION OF CHEESES—HARD AND FRESH COMPARED
(PER 100 GRAMS OF CHEESE)

COMPONENT	PARMESAN (UNGRATED)	CHEDDAR	EDAM	FETA	COTTAGE CHEESE (2% MILKFAT)
Water (% of total weight)	29.2	36.8	46	55	79.3
Protein (% of total weight)	35.8	24.9	25	14.2	13.7
Fat (% of total weight)	25.8	33.1	22	22	1.9
Cholesterol (mg)	68	105	89	89	8
Energy (kcal)	392	412	357	264	90

CHEESE-MAKING OVERVIEW

1. Heat fresh milk.

2. Add starter culture (bacteria) to acidify the milk.

3. Let the acidified milk thicken, or set.

4. Add rennet (an enzyme) to solidify the proteins and to separate the liquid whey.

5. Cut the curds.

6. Heat and stir the curds, which expel water.

7. Drain the liquid whey. Curd particles will stick together, or knit.

8. Press the curds to remove even more liquid. Apply weight to the cheese to give it its final shape and to remove still more liquid.

9. Add salt by sprinkling or rubbing it onto the cheese or submerging the cheese in salt brine, which draws out more water.

10. Age the cheese to enhance its flavor and complexity (optional).

Now that you have a rough idea of the steps, we'll discuss in detail the techniques involved in the cheese-making process. Make sure you bookmark these pages: this chapter contains all of the information you'll need to master the recipes.

MILKING IT

Before you start on a recipe, you need to know how to handle the main ingredient: the milk. You also have to decide what kind of milk to use. Some recipes specify, but if you want to change it up a bit once you've mastered a recipe, here's what you'll need to know.

Temperature Conversion

Temperatures in this book are given only in Fahrenheit. Use the following equations to convert temperatures to Celcius:

♣ To convert Fahrenheit to Celsius: subtract 32, multiply by 5, and divide by 9.

♣ To convert Celsius to Fahrenheit: multiply by 9, divide by 5, and add 32.

A dairy thermometer ensures that milk reaches the correct temperature.

HEATING MILK

Unless the recipe calls for heating directly on the stove, use a double boiler or a water bath. A water bath is a sink full of water that is 10 degrees warmer than the target temperature of your milk. If the milk is too hot, remove the pot from the sink. If it's too cool, add hot water to the sink. Indirect heating allows for more even heat distribution and prevents scorching.

USING RAW UNPASTEURIZED MILK

Recipes in this book are based on pasteurized whole milk. If you are using raw unpasteurized milk (clean and tested), reduce the amounts of starter and rennet by half.

ADDING A STARTER CULTURE

As its name suggests, your starter culture begins the process of changing lactose (milk sugar) into lactic acid. This equalizes the pH so that the milk protein will form curds when rennet is added. Starter culture contains active lactic acid–producing bacteria, which acidify the milk, usually during the next thirty to sixty minutes. The increase in acidity must proceed at the right rate, and the level of milk acidity must not be too high or too low when you add rennet. Clabbered (over-acidified) milk will not yield a clean break (when the curd is ready, a knife can cleanly separate it).

TYPES OF STARTER CULTURES

There are two types of starter cultures: mesophilic and thermophilic.

A packet of Mesophilic culture.

❖ **Mesophilic culture** is used to make low-temperature cheese. (Soft cheeses and some hard cheeses cook at low temperatures.) It grows best when the temperature of the heated milk is 80 to 86 degrees Fahrenheit. At temperatures lower than 70 degrees Fahrenheit or higher than 86 degrees Fahrenheit, the bacteria don't work well. Temperatures above 104 degrees Fahrenheit destroy the bacteria.

❖ **Thermophilic culture** is used to make high-temperature cheese. (Italian and Swiss cheeses require high-temperature cooking.) It tolerates heat up to 132 degrees Fahrenheit. At temperatures lower than 86 degrees Fahrenheit, the bacteria are inactive.

REPLACING MILK IN RECIPES

Unless a recipe specifies goat's or sheep's milk, the recipes in this book are based on the use of whole cow's milk. But once you've mastered a recipe using cow's milk, you may want to substitute one kind of milk for another. If you do, keep these things in mind:

❖ Goat's milk is more acidic than cow's milk (it has a lower pH). You will need to reduce the amount of rennet by about a quarter. If a recipe calls for 1 teaspoon rennet, for example, use ³⁄₄ teaspoon instead. The reverse is true if you are substituting cow's milk for goat's milk.

❖ Sheep's milk has more milk solids than either cow's or goat's milk. Reduce the rennet by a quarter and plan on a higher yield.

Mesophilic and thermophilic cultures come prepackaged, but you can also make your own (see "Making Your Own Starter" on the opposite page). However, unless you plan to make cheese several times a week, you probably don't need a mother culture.

Direct-set culture saves time, is simple to use, and reduces possible milk contamination. There are direct-set cultures for all types of cheese, sold as a freeze-dried powder by cheese-making suppliers (see Resources, page 173). They can stay in your freezer unopened for up to two years. (*Note:* If you are buying direct-set starter in bulk, use these guidelines: ⅛ teaspoon per 1 gallon of milk, ¼ teaspoon per 2 to 5 gallons of milk, and ½ teaspoon per 5 to 10 gallons of milk.)

OUR FRIEND BACTERIA

Starter bacteria's role in cheese making is to fight harmful bacteria that want to spoil your milk. The *lactocci* and *lactobacilli* you add at this early stage are friendly bacteria, not the unfriendly pathogenic variety. As a society, we seem to be obsessed with germs, but life—and cheese making—would be unthinkable without beneficial microbes. As cheese maker and business owner Rory Chase says, "If our bodies were voting republics, we'd be ruled by bacteria." He and his business partner Peter Destler co-own the Amazing Real Live Food Co., which enhances its products with life-sustaining probiotics.

COLORING AND OTHER ADDITIVES

Milk color is determined by carotenes (natural pigments) and can vary depending on the animal and what it's eating. Goat's and sheep's milk, for example, are naturally white because they lack carotenes. Cheese makers often use safe nontoxic vegetable dyes to give their cheeses a rich yellow caste. The most popular vegetable dye is *annatto*, an extract from the seeds of *Bixa orellana*, a shrub native to Central and South America. In years past, carrot juice, saffron, and marigold petals were added for color. All of the following additives are available from cheese-making suppliers:

♣ **Annatto.** This is sold as a liquid and must be diluted before using. Two drops per gallon of milk in ¼ cup of water is usually enough. Add it before adding the rennet as it can weaken coagulation. Mix it thoroughly into the warm milk. Its color won't show until after you drain the curds.

♣ **Calcium Chloride.** Adding calcium chloride to pasteurized and homogenized milk restores calcium lost during the milk's heat treatment. Cheese makers also add it to compensate for seasonal variations in the milk. Use ¼ teaspoon calcium chloride per gallon of milk. Dilute the calcium chloride in ¼ cup of unchlorinated water, and add the mixture to the heated milk. After adding rennet, let the milk set 3 to 5 minutes longer than usual before cutting the curds.

♣ **Lipase powder.** This is an enzyme used to produce extra acid. If your recipe calls for it,

Making Your Own Starter

A *mother culture* is a homegrown starter that you can store and keep using indefinitely to make more batches. Follow these directions to make a mother culture using direct-set culture.

To make your first batch of mesophilic starter:

1. Boil a clean 1-quart canning jar and its lid in water for five minutes.

2. Remove and cool. Fill the jar with fresh skim milk, leaving ½ inch at the top. Screw the lid on tightly.

3. Place the jar in a deep pot so that the water covers the top of the lid.

4. Bring the pot of water to a boil, and continue at a slow boil for thirty minutes.

5. Remove the jar, and let the milk cool to 75 degrees Fahrenheit. (You will need a dairy thermometer to test temperature.)

6. Pour ¼ teaspoon freeze-dried mesophilic culture into the cooled sterilized milk. Cover the jar with the lid, and swirl to dissolve the powder.

7. Set the jar where it can be kept at 75 degrees Fahrenheit for about eighteen hours as the milk ripens.

8. The finished culture should have the consistency of yogurt (or buttermilk, if you're using goat's milk) and separate cleanly from the sides of the jar.

9. Chill the culture in the fridge right away. It will keep unopened for up to two weeks. To freeze your mother culture, sterilize plastic ice cube trays. Fill the trays, cover them with plastic wrap, and freeze them. Be sure to label the frozen cubes "mesophilic" with the date. They'll be good for up to three months. Each cube measures 1 ounce and can be thawed to make cheese or another batch of culture.

To make a thermophilic starter, follow steps 1 through 4 above, and then:

1. Remove the jar from the water and let the milk cool to 110 degrees Fahrenheit.

2. Pour ¼ teaspoon freeze-dried thermophilic culture into the cooled sterilized milk. Cover the jar with the lid, and swirl to dissolve the powder.

3. Set the jar in a pot of water heated to 110 degrees Fahrenheit, and keep it at that temperature for four to six hours. The milk should look like yogurt and separate cleanly from the sides of the jar. Follow step 9 above.

Troubleshooting Your Mother Culture

❖ If your starter won't coagulate, it may be because the room temperature is too low, the bacteria you added wasn't active, the residue of detergent or bleach on utensils interfered with bacterial action, or you didn't add enough powdered culture.

❖ Bubbles in your finished starter mean bad news. Either your equipment or the skim milk wasn't sterile. Toss it out and start over.

dissolve the powder in ¼ cup of cool water and let it sit for twenty minutes before adding it to your heated milk.

♣ **Ash.** A food-grade charcoal sprinkled on some cheeses, especially goat's milk cheeses, to protect them from unwanted mold growth as they ripen. Ash is also added to protect a layer of curd before more curd is added. This tradition continues with French cheeses such as Morbier and Cypress Grove's Humboldt Fog cheese from Arcata, California.

♣ **Bacteria and Molds.** We have seen how bacteria is added to milk to "start" acidification. Other bacteria and molds are added to develop a cheese's distinctive flavor.

♣ *Penicillium candidum.* A white mold, *Penicillium candidum* neutralizes acidity and prevents mold growth while it enhances flavor in soft-ripened cheeses such as Camembert and Brie. It can be added directly to milk or sprayed on the cheese's surface.

♣ *Geotrichum candidum.* This white mold is often used together with *P. candidum* or *Brevibacterium linens* to cure cheese. It can be added directly to milk or sprayed on the cheese's surface.

♣ *Penicillium roqueforti.* A blue mold, *Penicillium roqueforti* produces blue-green veins, sharp taste, and creamy consistency. It can be added directly to milk or sprayed on the cheese's surface.

♣ *Brevibacterium linens.* This is a ripening bacterium. It is added to milk and diluted in a brine that's rubbed on the cheese's surface to create an orange-red smear.

♣ **Propionic bacteria.** This type of bacteria is added to milk to create the signature holes and flavor of Swiss cheese.

ADDING A COAGULANT

By adding culture (friendly bacteria) and rennet, you are breaking down the chemical reactions that keep protein, fat, and minerals suspended in milk. The first of those reactions is milk sugar converting to lactic acid. Adding rennet causes a second chemical reaction. Rennet contains *chymosin*, a coagulating enzyme that acts on casein, separating milk into curds (solids) and whey (liquid). You can buy rennet at cheese-supply stores in liquid, tablet, and powdered form. Store liquid rennet in the fridge, tablets and powder in your freezer.

Until recently, rennet was derived from the stomach lining of a calf, goat, or lamb. Now, most cheese makers use vegetable or microbial rennets. In addition to being less expensive than traditional animal rennets, vegetable rennet allows cheese makers to craft a product vegans can eat. Vegetable rennet that's sold in stores contains an enzyme

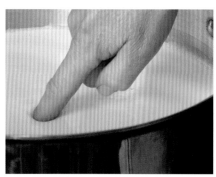
Coagulation creates a seemingly solid mass of curd.

derived from *Rhizomucor miehei* mold. Herbalists have experimented using nettles, butterwort leaves, knapweed, mallow, teasel, yarrow, and thistle flowers as coagulants.

DILUTING RENNET

Always dilute rennet (liquid, powder, or tablet) in cool unchlorinated water before adding it to the milk (¼ cup of water is enough for a 1- to 2-gallon recipe). If you're using powder or crushed tablet rennet, let it sit for forty minutes, stirring occasionally, until it's completely dissolved.

ADDING RENNET

Pour the diluted rennet into the milk and mix it gently using an up-and-down motion for about one minute (a circular motion is too hard to stop). Make sure to reach the bottom of your pot. If you are using creamline (unhomogenized) milk, top-stir it (stir just the top ¼ inch of the milk) to mix in any fat that's risen to the surface. Top-stirring ensures an even distribution of rennet. Cover the pot and let the milk set for the time specified in your recipe. Don't stir or move the pot once the milk has started to coagulate.

CHECKING FOR A CLEAN BREAK

After the rennet has worked on the ripened milk, you need to test to see if the curd mass has *set* (gelled). It's important to cut it at the right moment—too soon and the curd will be mushy, too late and it will be too firm. This test is called a *clean break*, and it involves placing a clean utensil into the curd at a 45-degree angle. If the curd separates cleanly, then it's ready to be cut. If it doesn't break cleanly but instead has a ragged split and the whey around it is milky, wait a few minutes and test it again. Another test is to pull the curd away from the side of the pot; it should resist.

Adding rennet.

Top-stirring.

Checking for a clean break.

CONCENTRATING ON CURDS

Depending on the cheese you're making, you will use various methods—cutting, cooking, pressing, milling, and salting—to concentrate the curd.

CUTTING CURDS

Once your curd has set, you will cut it into small cubes to allow the whey to drain. Cut the cubes as close as possible to the size your recipe calls for—curd size directly affects cheese texture. In addition to a long knife, cheese makers often use wire whisks to cut grain-size curd and skimmers to cut and lift curd.

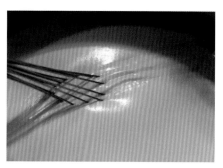
Cutting curds using a whisk.

Soft curds need no cutting. Ladle them *gently* into a mold or a butter muslin–lined colander per your recipe. Hard-cheese curd should be cut in the pot as follows (for this example, we'll assume the recipe has called for ½-inch curds):

1. Place your curd knife ½ inch from the left side of the pot. Draw your knife through the curd in a straight line, making sure to touch the bottom of the pot. Make another knife slice ½ inch to the right of the first. Continue to cut rows that are ½ inch apart.

2. Rotate the pot 90 degrees, and repeat the slicing from left to right at ½-inch intervals. You will have a pot of ½-inch square curds.

3. Use a skimmer to cut the curd horizontally, from side to side and from top to bottom.

4. After cutting, let the curd settle for five minutes, then gently stir, cutting any oversized cubes with the knife.

The goal at this stage is to release liquid trapped in the solid mass. Most hard-cheese recipes call for curds that measure ¼ to ½ inch. The smaller the curd particle, the less water it will hold.

Checking the temperature.

HEATING CURDS

Everything the cheese maker does from this point on is designed to squeeze whey out of the cheese curds. Remember that the harder the cheese, the less moisture it contains. Dry firm cheeses such as Parmigiano-Reggiano and Gruyère are cooked at very high temperatures and stirred for a long time to remove water.

After cutting, the cubes of curd release whey and begin to contract (this is called *synersis*). The next steps are to cook them to release more whey, to dry and firm them, and to increase acidity. Increase the heat gradually as you gently stir, and notice that the amount of whey increases. Stirring keeps the cubes you've cut from clumping together.

DRAINING CURDS

Some cheese makers use the following test to tell whether curd is ready to be drained:

1. Take a handful of curd cubes and press them gently to form a ball in your palm.
2. Rub the ball of curd with your thumb; the curds should stick together.

If the curds don't stick together, leave them in the whey for another five to ten minutes. Perform the test again.

Soft-cheese curds are placed in butter muslin (or tightly woven cheesecloth) and hung to drain, usually from six to twelve hours. Line a colander or strainer with muslin and gently ladle in the curds. Break as few as possible to conserve the milk solids and maximize the final yield. Tie the corners of the muslin into a knot, and hang the bag over a bowl in your sink. (The whey can be reused for ricotta within three hours, or you can refrigerate it for up to a week.)

Hard-cheese curds are drained for a shorter time. Line a colander with muslin and gently ladle in the curds. The whey should run clear at this point. After draining, most hard-cheese curds are broken up by hand, a process called *milling*.

Pouring curds and whey into a colander lined with butter muslin.

Draining curds over a colander.

Drained curds.

SAVING WHEY

The liquid left over after you drain the cheese curds is full of proteins, vitamins, and minerals. Why throw it away? It can be used to make whey cheeses such as ricotta (literally *recooked*), mysost, and gjetost. You will need at least 2 gallons of whey to make ricotta and, although fresh whey is best, it will keep refrigerated for up to one week. Whey is also delicious in bread recipes and as a soup stock, and you can use it to cook pasta or beans as well. Traditionally, farmers fed whey to their pigs to fatten them up. (*Note:* You can't make ricotta with whey from acid-precipitated cheese such as paneer and mozzarella.)

Salting the curds.

SALTING CURDS

Salt adds to the cheese's flavor and helps prevent the growth of unfriendly bacteria. It also draws moisture from the curds, causing them to shrink and expel more whey. Not just any salt will do for cheese making; it must be noniodized, such as Kosher salt. Salt is usually added to curds just before they are pressed, rubbed onto a cheese after its rind has formed, or used to make a saturated brine that the cheese can soak in. Let's look at each of these techniques:

❖ **Mixing.** For soft cheese, remove curd from the muslin bag, add salt to taste, and mix. For hard cheese, sprinkle on the salt according to your recipe, and mix.

❖ **Rubbing.** Rub salt on mold-ripened cheese before it is dried and aged.

❖ **Soaking.** Hard cheese, such as Gouda and feta, are put into a brine bath *after pressing*. The amount of salt in the bath depends on the cheese. To make a saturated (heavily salted) solution, stir 2 pounds of Kosher salt into 1 gallon of nearly boiling (190 degrees Fahrenheit) water. Once the salt has dissolved, let the water chill. The first time you make the brine bath, add 1 tablespoon of calcium chloride per gallon of water—it prevents the salt from leaching calcium out of the cheese. To reuse your brine, boil it, add more salt until it no longer dissolves, let the brine cool, and refrigerate it.

MOLDING CURDS

Once the cheese has been salted, it's ready to be put into molds and pressed. Because the mold determines the shape of your cheese, select it carefully. Line it with cheesecloth. Then place the curds into the mold—lightly for cheese that will be pressed lightly or not at all, firmly for hard cheese that will be heavily pressed. Place the mold on a drip tray so that the whey can drain.

PRESSING CURDS

Cheese is pressed to squeeze out more whey and compress the curd. (Depending on the type of cheese, you may need to buy a press specifically made for this purpose.) The amount of pressure and duration will determine the cheese's texture. Remember to apply pressure gradually so as not to lose butterfat. If your runoff is colored, not clear, release the pressure. Follow these steps to press your curds:

1. Wait until the temperature of your curds has fallen to at least 70 degrees Fahrenheit before pressing.

2. Put the curd-filled mold on a drip tray so that the whey can drain into your sink or into a bowl. Raise it using a cheese board (a board used to drain soft cheese) if you need more height.

3. Cover the top of the curd in the mold with excess cheesecloth, and cover that with a *follower* (lid) that fits the mold. Pull the cloth tight.

4. Apply pressure lightly for the first fifteen minutes.

5. Remove the mold from the press and the cheese from the mold.

6. Peel the cheesecloth off and turn the cheese over; cover with the same cloth. This process is called *redressing*, and it allows for more equal pressing.

7. Replace the cheese in the mold, cloth on top of it, and follower on top of that.

8. Press the cheese according to the recipe's directions. It is usually left in the press under full pressure for at least twelve hours.

A cheese press.

Curds inside of the press.

Pressed cheese.

Recipes for hard cheeses use the following gauge:

❖ Light pressure = 5 to 10 psi

❖ Medium pressure = 10 to 20 psi

❖ Firm pressure = 20 to 45 psi or higher

Psi means "pounds per square inch," so the weight is divided over the surface area. If you're pressing two cheeses under one weight, you must double the recommended pressure.

Lactose Intolerance versus Milk Allergies

If you love cheese but are lactose intolerant, all is not lost. There are several options: First, you can start by making aged hard cheeses, which have less lactose than soft cheeses. Or try goat's milk cheese, which is naturally lower in lactic acid. Yogurt cheese contains bacteria that aids in the digestion of milk, so this is another option. Finally, if needed, you can add lactase to the cheese you make. Following the directions on the package, add the product to your milk; let the milk sit in the refrigerator for twenty-four hours before you make cheese with it.

On the other hand, some people have a reaction to the proteins, not the lactose, in milk. Symptoms range from a runny nose, itching, and watery eyes to more severe symptoms such as skin rash and vomiting. Fortunately for the cheese lover, an allergy to cow's milk doesn't necessarily mean an allergy to goat's or sheep's milk. Check with a specialist to see if you are allergic and, if so, to which type of milk. Milk allergies are important to diagnose and not as easily remedied as lactose intolerance.

THE FINAL STEPS

The goal of this stage is to ripen (or age) the prepared cheese, and the cheese maker's role is to manipulate natural chemical changes using temperature and humidity. Those chemical changes determine the finished cheese's flavor, texture, and aroma.

Air-drying cheese under a food net.

AIR-DRYING

Remove the pressed cheese from the mold, and peel away the cheesecloth. Place the cheese on a cheese board or mat until it is dry to the touch—this usually takes several days. Turn the cheese over periodically, per your recipe, to ensure that all of its surfaces dry thoroughly. You want a natural rind, not mold, to form. If mold appears, clean the outside of your cheese using cheesecloth soaked in vinegar or salted water. (To make a simple brine, dissolve 1 teaspoon of Kosher salt into ½ cup boiled water. Let cool.)

BANDAGING

Cloth bandaging protects the inside of an aging cheese while still allowing it to breathe. It's the traditional way to form a rind on Cheddar and more effective in curing the cheese than waxing.

1. Place the round of cheese on a clean sheet of cheesecloth.
2. Trace the circumference of the round, and cut four circles wide enough to cover the sides of the round.
3. Rub a thin coat of vegetable shortening all over the cheese.
4. Lay cheesecloth on the top and bottom of the round, and seal it to the sides. Smooth the cloth to eliminate air pockets.

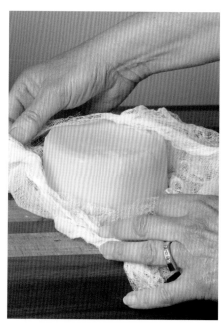
Bandaging cheese in cheesecloth.

5. Repeat the process so two layers of cheesecloth protect all sides of the round.

Store the cheese at the temperature and humidity indicated in the recipe. A rind will form on the outside of the bandage and will be stripped away when the cheese is ready to be cut, in three to six months.

WAXING

Waxing is also used to prevent excess drying and to retard mold. It's an especially smart solution if you aren't able to control the humidity of your ripening box as the cheese ages. Be sure to use cheese wax, which is softer than paraffin wax. Here are the steps for waxing cheese:

Dipping cheese in wax.

1. Melt the cheese wax in a double boiler. Reserve a pie tin or pot just for waxing so that you can store the extra and reuse it.

2. Holding the cheese on the top and bottom with your fingertips, roll it in the hot wax to coat all sides. Set it on parchment paper to dry.

3. When the sides are dry, dip the top and bottom, allowing the wax to dry between coats. I find that painting the wax onto the cheese with a natural-bristle brush is much easier. Apply two to three coats of wax, which dry quickly.

4. Label the cheese with its name and the date. You can wax the paper onto the surface.

Note: To reuse old cheese wax, melt and strain it through a piece of butter muslin.

DOUBLING RECIPES

If you need more cheese than the recipe calls for, you can increase the ingredients proportionately. This will be easier once you've made the cheese and liked the result. Look at your notes regarding setting and coagulation times. You may have to reduce the amount of rennet you add. You may also have to adjust the temperature, remembering that if the temperature is too high, it may kill the bacteria or your rennet enzyme. If the temperature is too low, it may inhibit the bacteria's growth and the rennet's activity.

AGING

This is the true test of a hard cheese. During its maturation, a cheese must be exposed to the proper temperature and humidity so that friendly bacteria (introduced by the starter) can make enough acidity to preserve (not rot) your cheese. Stick to the instructions in the recipe.

Soft cheese is typically not aged. As for hard cheese, most of us don't have an underground cave on our properties or an aging room where we can adjust temperature and humidity. Hard cheese needs a constant temperature of 50 to 55 degrees Fahrenheit and a relative humidity between 65 and 85 percent, depending on the cheese. Too cold and the acid won't develop, too warm and you may be growing mold spores.

Cool basements, cellars, and cold rooms are ideal ripening areas. You can also buy a small

A cheese cave.

fridge, place a pan of water on the bottom, and adjust the temperature setting. To complete your homemade "cheese cave," you will need a thermometer/hygrometer, which is easy to find at a hardware store.

Most refrigerators are set at 40 degrees Fahrenheit, which is too cold and dry to age cheese. But I've had good luck aging cheese in airtight plastic containers set on the bottom of the fridge, either in or in place of vegetable bins. I place a sanitized wet sponge (to maintain moisture) in the ripening box and monitor temperature and humidity with a combination thermometer/hygrometer. If you see moisture collecting on the lid or bottom, wipe it off when you turn your cheese. Pay close attention to moisture buildup as it can become a breeding ground for mold.

Turn the cheese over every day for the first few weeks, then several times a week. If moisture gathers under the cheese, it may rot. The longer your cheese ages, the stronger its flavor. Some of the grating cheeses, such as Romano, are aged for years to give them a real bite. Patience, in this case, means good eating.

Some people test cheese using a *cheese trier* (a device specifically used to test cheese) during aging to check flavor, aroma, moisture, acidity, and other features. Push the trier into the side of your cheese, and turn it completely once or twice. The drier the cheese, the more resistance you'll feel. Withdraw the plug of cheese, and pick off a piece with your clean fingers to taste. Replace the plug and seal the hole with some of the cheese sample to prevent mold from entering. Continue aging if it's not ready.

TESTING ACIDITY

Maintain a comfortable temperature and those friendly bacteria will munch on lactose sugar, converting it to lactic acid. Because proper acid buildup is essential to a cheese's flavor, texture, and safe preservation (for hard cheeses), you may want to test for it. There are three ways to test:

❧ Compare pH strips to a color chart. The pH scale measures the concentration of hydrogen ions in milk—its acidity or alkalinity. A value of 7.0 is neutral. Values above 7.0 mean that the milk is alkaline; anything below 7.0 means it's acidic. Fresh cheese is more acidic, for example, because it contains more lactic acid than hard cheese. (You can buy pH strips at drugstores.)

❧ Add a few drops of phenolphthalein (colorless) to your milk to test for titrated acidity (TA). If the milk is acidic, it will remain colorless. If it is alkaline, its color will turn pink. Acid-testing kits are available from cheese-making suppliers.

❧ You can buy a pH meter, but they are not cheap. They consist of a special measuring probe (a glass electrode) connected to an electronic meter that measures and displays the pH reading.

Storing cheese.

STORING CHEESE

Hard cheese, if properly aged, stays fresh for months in your refrigerator. Soft cheese will last only about two weeks. Keep cheeses cool, between 38 and 42 degrees Fahrenheit, in a vegetable bin at the bottom of your fridge. Wrap your cut cheese in aluminum foil, wax paper, or plastic wrap. If it gets moldy, trim away the mold and wrap the unspoiled chunk in a new piece of foil or plastic. If a hard cheese becomes cracked and dry, wrap it for several hours in a damp towel. The cheese you've created is a living, breathing organism that continues to ripen until you eat it.

Increasing Your Yield

Here are a few tips to help you increase a yield:

❧ Use whole milk. Skim or low-fat milk will reduce the amount of finished cheese.

❧ If you're using homogenized/ pasteurized milk, add ⅛ teaspoon calcium chloride per 2 gallons of milk. Remember to dilute the calcium chloride in ¼ cup cool unchlorinated water. Though my recipes don't call for it, adding calcium chloride restores some calcium ions lost during heat treatment.

❧ Be gentle handling the curd. The more it breaks down, the more milk solids are lost in the whey.

CONCLUSION

As you can see, a skilled artisan can manipulate milk's chemistry to create any number of delicious cheeses. The magic is limited only by imagination and, perhaps, tenacity.

Colin McGrath makes about 40,000 pounds of cheese a year at Sprout Creek Farm near Poughkeepsie, New York. He has an intuitive style he describes as "70 percent feel, 30 percent science." Each batch of cheese is invariably different for McGrath, who treats the process creatively, leaving the door open for accidents and improvisation. "I respect tradition," he says, "but I'm not bound by it."

Unrestricted by the *Appellation d'Origine Contrôlée* (AOC) certification system that governs wine and cheese in France, you can follow your artistic instincts as McGrath does.

All good things need time to ripen—including cheese and your mastery of the techniques discussed in this chapter. Careful attention to these guidelines may reduce that learning curve:

1. Stick to the recipe until you've mastered it—then you can get creative.

2. Always sterilize your equipment and keep work areas spotless. You want those friendly bacteria to have a chance to work for you, not against you.

3. Keep records. If the batch is a success, you'll want to repeat it. If not, you'll know what to avoid next time. I encourage you to make copies of the Cheese Diary on page 166, or create your own.

CHAPTER 4

Before You Begin

To become an artisan cheese maker, you'll need to know what you're working with and how to use it. Before Fahrenheit invented his thermometer, people often tested milk temperature by dipping an elbow in the simmering pot. As science became the norm, recipes became more precise and the finished cheese more predictable. You will have most of the tools for home cheese making, such as a stainless-steel pot and ladle, already in your kitchen. You can purchase other items from a cheese-making supplier as you need them (see Resources, page 173).

> "Cheese making is babysitting. It's very labor-intensive."
> —Sadie Kendall, Kendall Farms

Just as important as using the proper tools is sanitizing those tools and your workspace. You don't have to be a slave to cleanliness, but you do need to start off with a clean slate, so to speak. And as with any cooking project, attention to detail ensures delicious results.

EQUIPMENT

If you are a beginner, start with recipes for fresh cheeses that require no pressing or aging. More advanced cheese making requires more advanced tools. The following are the essential items you can't make cheese without:

❖ **Colander or 8-inch strainer.** You will line this with cheesecloth to drain your curds. I prefer a colander with high feet.

❖ **Cooking pots.** Stainless steel, glass, or enamel pots are useful because they are easy to keep clean and will not react with acid created during the cheese-making process. You

don't want your beloved curds to taste metallic, as they might if you use cast-iron or aluminum. For the recipes in this book, your pot must be large enough to hold 2 gallons of milk. I prefer an enamel pot or a stainless steel one with a thick aluminum bottom to prevent scorching. For indirect heating, you will need two pots that fit inside each other (a double boiler works well) or you can place the cheese pot in a sink of warm water.

Cheesecloth lining a colander.

A colander within a catch bowl.

A knife for cutting curds.

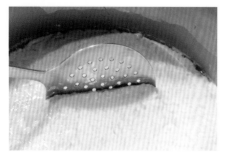
A skimmer for top-stirring and cutting.

❖ **Cheesecloth.** Use cheesecloth to drain curds or line molds for hard cheese. Buy professional-quality cheesecloth, which has a tight weave and can be washed, sanitized, and used again. To reuse it, rinse it in cold water, wash it with a little bleach, and then boil it.

❖ **Butter muslin.** This cloth has a tighter weave than cheesecloth and can be cleaned and reused like cheesecloth. Either of these is a must if you don't want to lose your curds down the drain.

❖ **Catch bowl and catch pan.** These are used to collect whey (any nonplastic bowl that can be sterilized will do).

❖ **Knife.** You'll need one that's at least 10 inches long with a thin blade to cut curds. Choose one that reaches the bottom of the pot. Professional curd knives have a flat tip, rather than a pointed one.

❖ **Measuring cup.** Use one that's glass, not plastic.

❖ **Measuring spoons.** Stainless steel is preferable.

❖ **Perforated ladle,** also called a **skimmer**. You will use this to stir milk, cut curd, and transfer curd into molds. As with all utensils, stainless steel is best.

❖ **Thermometer.** Any thermometer with a range from 0 to 220 degrees Fahrenheit will do; a candy thermometer's range is too high. Dairy thermometers that float or attach to the pot's side are most convenient.

Those are the essentials, but as you become more ambitious in your experiments, you'll want to invest in more tools. Here's a list of the equipment you may need as you delve further into the cheese-making universe:

❖ **Cutting boards.** A simple cutting board of unfinished wood is perfect to drain and air-dry soft cheeses because it absorbs moisture from the bottom of the cheese. Don't use plastic, as it will not absorb moisture.

❖ **Cheese trier.** This simple stainless-steel tool is used to core out a sample from the cheese's center—a test for ripeness that doesn't require cutting a wedge.

❖ **Cheese wrap.** This is a type of cellophane used to protect soft and mold-ripened cheeses during storage. You want a breathable covering, not plastic wrap.

❖ **Combination thermometer/hygrometer.** You'll use this to measure the temperature and humidity of your *ripening cave* (see page 54).

❖ **Draining rack.** You want one that fits inside your plastic container, such as a cake rack.

❖ **Mats.** These are also used for draining and air-drying. Bamboo sushi mats will do, or you could use ones made of food-grade plastic. Have at least two mats on hand.

❖ **Molds and followers**. Molds hold curds and give the cheese a shape. They come in all shapes and sizes and range from 10-pound molds for Emmental to tiny Crottin cups. You can make your own by choosing a food-grade plastic container and punching holes into the bottom and sides. Followers are flat disks that fit inside the molds and press the curds evenly when weight is applied. A follower needs to be slightly smaller in diameter than the mold. You can improvise with wooden followers; plastic followers tend to split.

❖ **pH testing equipment.** As described in chapter 3, the three options for testing milk acidity are: (1) pH strips, (2) phenol-phthalein, and (3) an instant-read battery-operated meter. Price difference? A few dollars to a few hundred dollars.

❖ **Plastic sealable containers.** These are for draining and ripening cheese. A good size is 14 by 20 by 7 inches.

❖ **Press.** A press is crucial for making hard cheese. As you apply pressure to cheese in a perforated mold, whey drains and the curd solidifies. Other than a ripening cave, a cheese press will be your greatest investment. You can make

A dairy thermometer.

A digital dairy thermometer.

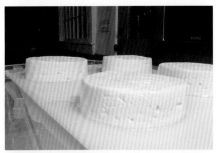
Cheese on a draining board.

Cheese in molds, draining.

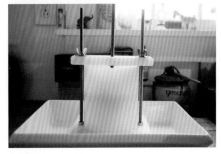
A cheese press.

do with a *tomme mold* (a hard plastic mold and lid with small holes in the sides and bottom) weighted down with barbells, but eventually you will want a cheese press with a pressure gauge. Supply houses offer a variety of them, but you can be thrifty and fashion your own. New England Cheesemaking Supply Company sells its "Off-the-Wall" press plans, which help you make a lever-type press at home.

❖ **Ripening cave.** How do you simulate the damp, cool atmosphere of a limestone cave in your home? A cellar or unheated room is ideal if its year-round temperature is about 55 degrees Fahrenheit. Otherwise, you can buy a small fridge or wine cooler and manually set the temperature that your recipe calls for. Humidity can be adjusted using a sponge or pan of water and monitored using a hygrometer.

Saving Energy

You can "green" your kitchen by buying Energy-Star-qualified appliances. These heating (stove) and cooling (refrigerator) sources use about 40 percent less energy than appliances made before 2001. Traditional methods of cheese making used even less electric energy. Cooking your curd on a woodstove, reusing whey and other ingredients, and aging cheese in a cellar or other cold room will all help reduce demand on the commercial grid.

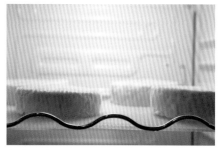
A ripening cave.

Wax being melted.

❖ **Ripening paper.** You'll wrap some cheeses in ripening paper, which uses an absorbent inner layer to soak up moisture from the cheese's surface, while an outer layer protects the cheese from losing excessive moisture to the air.

❖ **Wax brush and pan.** A natural-bristle brush, not a nylon one, is best. Reserve it just for coating your finished cheese with wax. The same is true for your wax pan.

❖ **Wax.** Wax creates a protective coating that guards against bacteria and dryness during the aging process. Professional-quality cheese wax is reusable.

THE IMPORTANCE OF CLEANLINESS

Cheese making requires meticulous sanitation to ensure the final product is savory and safe. "People go into it starry-eyed," says Jeffrey Roberts, author of *The Atlas of American Artisan Cheese*, "but they very quickly learn this is a lot of work." Colin McGrath, cheese maker at Sprout Creek Farm in Poughkeepsie, New York, is one of many who would vigorously agree. "I am a glorified janitor. I spend more time cleaning than making cheese."

STERILIZATION

Glass, stainless-steel, or food-grade plastic tools are recommended for a good reason: they can be sterilized. Porous materials—disposable plastic or wood—are hard to clean. So the first step before making *any* cheese is to sanitize all of your equipment. Here are some tips on how to do so:

Save your wooden cutting board specifically for draining soft cheeses or serving your finished products.

❖ Boil your utensils in a pot for five minutes, or steam them for five minutes in 2 inches of water in a large kettle with a tight lid. Steam or boil mats for at least twenty minutes between uses. Scrub and air-dry wooden boards.

❖ Dip food-grade plastic tools in a solution of 2 tablespoons of bleach per 1 gallon of water. Wipe work areas down with the same bleach solution.

❖ Clean large pans, molds, and colanders in the dishwasher right before using them.

While making cheese, rinse in cold water any utensils that touch milk, and then wash them in hot water. I always keep a pot of gently boiling water on the stove to resanitize utensils.

FOOD SAFETY

Cheese is safe to eat as a rule, but it does have the potential to produce serious illness. The risk of pathogen growth decreases as (1) pH decreases, (2) salt content increases, and (3) moisture content decreases. What this means is that the longer a cheese ripens, the less likely it will cause problems. Soft cheeses—bloomy-rind and washed-rind varieties—are especially vulnerable to pathogens; hard, long-aged cheeses such as Parmigiano-Reggiano carry almost no risk.

Play it safe, but don't be obsessive. As one professional said, "Relax. We're making cheese here, not running an operating room." Amen. Our standards of sanitation are light years more advanced than those of traditional cheese crafters in other parts of the world.

RECORD KEEPING

Some heavenly cheeses sold today were happy accidents. If you don't have a record of the steps you took in making a cheese, you'll never know how to recreate it—or how to do it differently if you hated the result. All professional cheese makers keep careful records for that reason. Your notes will include details about time, amount, and temperature for each step in the process—adding starter, adding rennet, and so on. So make sure that your clock, thermometer, and measuring tools are accurate. The Cheese Diary at the back of this book can serve as a guide.

CHAPTER 5

Soft Unripened Cheese

Fresh cheeses are the place for a beginning cheese maker to start. Mascarpone, cottage cheese, crème fraîche, ricotta, cream cheese, paneer, and Neufchatel can all be made and eaten the same day. They demand neither lots of time nor special equipment. Most will require a direct-set starter, but some—such as paneer—use acid (lemon juice) to coagulate the curd.

Because fresh cheese has mild (not tangy or sharp) flavors, I encourage you to spice it up with herbs, honey, fruits, or vegetables. The recipes in this chapter include those suggestions. Remember that these cheeses need to be enjoyed when they're fresh, usually in a day or two.

> "Cheese— milk's leap toward immortality."
>
> —Clifton Fadiman, American media personality and author

Unlike hard cheese, soft cheese has high whey or moisture content. Many are called "bag cheeses" because you use a butter-muslin bag to drain curds. The yield from 1 gallon of milk is about $1\frac{1}{2}$ to 2 pounds of soft cheese, depending on the type of milk you use. The greater the butterfat, the higher the cheese yield.

Review the steps for warming milk, adding starter, and draining curds in chapters 3 and 4. Fresh cheese doesn't usually require curd cutting, pressing in molds, or aging.

EQUIPMENT

To make the recipes for fresh cheese included in this chapter, you'll need the following tools:

❖ A stainless steel pot or double boiler

❖ A dairy thermometer with a range from 0 to 220 degrees Fahrenheit

❖ A stainless steel stirring spoon

❖ A colander or 8-inch strainer

❖ Butter muslin or tight-weave cheesecloth

❖ A catch bowl

❖ A tomme or 1-quart basket mold

Recipes that Come in Handy

Butter

Churning butter on the farm was a way to preserve the fat in milk before it spoiled. Cream was agitated until the butterfat was released, leaving—you guessed it—buttermilk. The taste of homemade butter will make you a believer. This simple recipe replaces hand churning with jar shaking. There are no penalties for using a food processor instead of a Mason jar. You can also skip the salt if you want unsalted butter (for example, for ghee).

Yield: 8 ounces

Ingredients:

❖ 1 pint pasteurized heavy cream

❖ Kosher salt

1. Leave the cream at room temperature for several hours to ripen.

2. Pour the cream into a sterilized 1-quart canning jar and screw on the lid.

3. Shake vigorously (or mix with a food processor) until the liquid separates from the solids. The cream will change from frothy white to pale yellow.

4. Pour the mixture into a fine-mesh strainer with a bowl beneath it to catch the buttermilk. (Save the buttermilk for drinking or for recipes such as buttermilk pancakes.)

5. Run cold tap water over the solids in the strainer, and then press with the bottom of a glass or a spoon to expel more buttermilk. Do this until the liquid runs clear.

6. Add salt to taste. The butter will keep refrigerated for about 2 weeks.

Ghee

Ghee is also called drawn butter or clarified butter. You will be removing milk solids, which makes the butter heat-tolerant and ideal for sautéing.

Yield: 1½ cups

Ingredients:

❖ 1 pound unsalted butter

1. Place the butter in a heavy saucepan over moderate heat. Swirl the pot as it heats so that the butter heats slowly and doesn't brown.
2. Increase the heat and bring the butter to a boil.
3. When it foams, stir gently and reduce the heat to the lowest possible setting.
4. Simmer uncovered and undisturbed for 45 minutes until the milk solids in the pan's bottom have turned golden brown and the ghee on top is transparent.
5. Strain the ghee through a muslin-lined strainer.
6. Pour the ghee into a jar and seal it tightly. The ghee should be perfectly clear.
7. Refrigerate. Ghee will keep for about 1 month.

Sour Cream

In this recipe, it's important that the ingredients be at room temperature and not ultra-pasteurized. The cultured buttermilk acts as a starter.

Yield: about 3 cups

Ingredients:

❖ 1 cup pasteurized heavy cream

❖ 1½ cups pasteurized whole milk

❖ ½ cup cultured buttermilk (not ultra-pasteurized)

1. Mix the ingredients together in a bowl.
2. Cover and let stand where the temperature is at least 70 degrees Fahrenheit for 12 to 24 hours. It should have the consistency of thick custard.
3. Refrigerate until ready to use (up to a week).

Paneer

Paneer is a staple in Indian cooking. Most Indian restaurants serve saag paneer, a savory blend of spinach, cumin, ghee, red chili powder, garlic, and coriander. This paneer has a much creamier texture than the commercial variety, though it's not as creamy as cottage cheese.

Yield: 1 pound

Ingredients:

❖ 1 gallon pasteurized whole milk

❖ 6 tablespoons lemon juice, or 2 teaspoons citric acid dissolved in ¾ cup hot water

1. Bring the milk to a gentle boil over direct medium heat. Stir often to prevent scorching.

2. Reduce the heat to low, add the lemon juice (or citric acid), and stir. The milk should start to separate into fluffy white curds and watery whey. If curds aren't forming, add more juice until the whey is almost clear.

3. Once the curd separates, remove the pot from the heat. If you want firmer curd, let it set for 5 to 10 minutes. For softer curd, drain right away.

4. Sterilize a piece of butter muslin about 20 square inches in size (you need enough extra to tie around the cheese). Line a colander with the cloth and place a catch bowl under the colander.

5. Ladle the curd into the colander.

6. Tie the corners of the muslin into a knot and gently twist to remove extra whey.

7. Return the cheese bag to your colander and place a plate or small cutting board on top. Put a 4-pound weight on top of that (a full half-gallon plastic water bottle weighs 4 pounds).

8. Let the weight press the cheese for 2 to 3 hours or until it has a firm consistency.

9. Unwrap the cheese and rinse the butter muslin in cold water. You can boil the muslin, adding a bit of baking soda, and reuse it later.

Saag Paneer

Paneer can be salted and flavored with herbs. It's a popular Indian dish in which the cheese absorbs a collection of spices. This is my favorite variation of the traditional recipe.

Yield: 6 servings

Ingredients:

- ¼ cup ghee (see page 59 for the recipe)
- 1 pound paneer, cut into ½-inch cubes
- ¼ cup onion, finely chopped
- 3 cloves garlic, peeled and crushed
- 1 tablespoon ginger, freshly grated
- 2 teaspoons ground coriander
- 1 teaspoon cumin
- 1 teaspoon red chili powder
- 1½ pounds fresh baby spinach, blanched, drained, and chopped
- 4 ounces heavy cream or buttermilk
- Salt

1. Heat the ghee in a skillet over a medium flame.
2. Add the cubed paneer and fry it until all sides are golden brown, turning them gently.
3. Remove the cheese using a slotted spoon and set it aside.
4. Sauté the onions, garlic, and ginger until soft.
5. Add spices and stir to marry the flavors.
6. Fold in the chopped spinach (make sure the spinach is well drained).
7. Cook for 4 to 5 minutes, and then add the paneer cubes.
8. Remove the skillet from the heat, and stir in the cream or buttermilk.
9. Add salt to taste.

Chèvre

Chèvre to a Frenchman means "goat." Not surprisingly, this word has become synonymous with "goat cheese." This simple recipe makes a creamy spread to which you can add fresh herbs and spices. You can also substitute chèvre for cream cheese or ricotta in pies and pasta dishes. Chèvre can be drained in a bag or molded. If you're making your own cheese molds, keep in mind that they should be made out of noncorrosive food-grade materials. Chèvre is delicious when melted with tomato and herbs on multigrain bread or mixed with artichokes and scallions as a spread.

Yield: 2 pounds

Ingredients:

❖ 1 gallon pasteurized whole goat's milk

❖ ¼ teaspoon direct-set mesophilic culture (Flora Danica starter is a good choice) or 4 tablespoons mesophilic mother culture

❖ 1 drop of liquid rennet dissolved in 3 tablespoons unchlorinated water

❖ Kosher salt

1. In a stainless steel pot, warm the milk to 80 degrees Fahrenheit.

2. Add the culture and let stand for 2 minutes to rehydrate. Mix well using a skimmer in an up-and-down motion.

3. Add 1 tablespoon of the diluted rennet and stir for 2 minutes.

4. Cover the milk and place the pot where it can sit undisturbed at 72 degrees Fahrenheit for about 12 hours. (I place mine in an unheated oven overnight.)

5. If the curd has set (you'll notice that the whey has risen, and a thin layer of cream rests on top of the goat's milk), check for a clean break (see chapter 3, page 41).

6. When the curd has set, cut it into ½-inch bits to release more whey.

7. Ladle the curds very gently into a colander lined with butter muslin with a catch bowl underneath (or into molds on a rack over a baking pan).

8. Tie the four ends of the muslin to create a ball and hang it over your sink. When the whey stops draining, the cheese is ready (usually in 4 to 6 hours).

9. Unwrap (or unmold) your cheese, and sprinkle all sides with a little Kosher salt.

10. Store leftover cheese (if there is any) in an airtight container in the refrigerator for up to 1 week.

Chèvre Chaud

The French find this hot goat cheese lunch irresistible. You will too.

Yield: 2 servings

Ingredients:

- ½ pound chèvre
- 1 egg, beaten
- ½ cup fresh bread crumbs (not processed)

1. Mold the chèvre into two thick patties.
2. Dip each patty into the beaten egg and coat with crumbs.
3. Place the chèvre patties on a nonstick baking sheet and broil until lightly browned.
4. Turn them over and brown the other side. The center of each should be soft.
5. Remove and serve on a bed of mixed greens with vinaigrette dressing on the side.

Linguini with Bay Scallops, Chèvre, and Red Peppers

Yield: 2 to 3 servings

Ingredients:

- ½ pound fresh linguini
- 3 tablespoons butter
- ½ cup chopped leeks
- ½ cup red bell peppers, thinly sliced
- 8 ounces bay scallops
- 6 ounces chèvre
- 2 tablespoons cream
- Salt, pepper, and cayenne
- Parsley, other herbs

1. Cook and drain the linguini.
2. Sauté the leeks and peppers in 2 tablespoons of butter until tender.
3. Add 1 tablespoon of butter and stir in the scallops. Sauté until the scallops are opaque, about 1 minute. Add the chèvre and cream, stir, and remove from heat.
4. Add salt, pepper, and cayenne to taste. Add the linguini to the warm pan and toss.
5. Sprinkle with chopped parsley and other herbs to taste. Serve immediately.

Feta

Unlike chèvre, this popular goat's milk cheese is heavily salted. Crumble it on your favorite salad, or cook with it. Goat's milk naturally contains lipase, but adding a bit more of this enzyme gives this cheese its "feta flavor." If you're making the recipe using cow's milk, add ¼ teaspoon lipase powder diluted in ¼ cup water. You will also need a tomme or 1-quart basket mold.

Yield: 1½ pounds

Ingredients:

❖ 1 gallon pasteurized whole goat's milk

❖ ¼ teaspoon direct-set mesophilic culture or 4 tablespoons mesophilic mother culture

❖ ½ teaspoon liquid rennet (or ½ of a rennet tablet), added with the lipase

❖ ⅛ teaspoon lipase powder, diluted in ¼ cup water and allowed to sit for 20 minutes

❖ 2 to 3 tablespoons Kosher salt

Brine (optional)

❖ ⅓ cup Kosher salt

❖ 1 teaspoon calcium chloride

❖ ½ gallon water

1. In a double boiler or water bath (see chapter 3, page 36), warm milk to 86 degrees Fahrenheit.

2. Add the culture and let it dissolve for 2 minutes. Use a skimmer to mix well using a top-to-bottom motion.

3. Cover and let the milk ripen for 1 hour at 86 degrees Fahrenheit.

4. Add rennet to the diluted lipase, and stir the mixture gently into the milk for a few minutes.

5. Cover and let set for 45 minutes at 86 degrees Fahrenheit or until the curd gives a clean break.

6. Cut the curd into ½-inch cubes, and allow the cubes to rest for 10 minutes.

7. Stir the curd gently, cutting any pieces you missed. Keep the curd at 86 degrees Fahrenheit for 20 minutes, stirring occasionally to prevent the pieces from sticking together. The curd will toughen as it releases whey and sink to the pot bottom.

8. Line your colander with a piece of damp butter muslin. Place a bowl or pot beneath the colander to catch the whey, which you can reuse. Pour in your curd, and let it drain for 5 minutes.

9. Break up the curd with your fingers, and mix in the Kosher salt.

10. Place a mold on a mat in a draining pan and fill it with curd. Let it drain for 1 hour, emptying whey from the pan and flipping the cheese in the mold every 15 minutes. (Hold the mold between 2 mats and turn it over.) After the first supervised hour, continue to let the cheese drain for 12 hours or until it's firm.

11. Remove the cheese from the mold. It's ready to eat now, but you can place it in brine for a stronger flavor. Let it soak in brine for 3 days, covered and at room temperature. Feta will keep refrigerated for up to 1 month.

Spanakopita

This popular Greek pastry is layered with spinach, savory feta cheese, onions, eggs, and seasonings, all wrapped in phyllo dough and toasted until the cheese melts. This recipe adds ricotta to the feta (see page 73 for the recipe).

Yield: 6 servings

Ingredients:

- 3 tablespoons olive oil
- 1 onion, chopped
- ½ cup green onions, chopped
- 2 cloves garlic, minced
- 2 pounds baby spinach, trimmed and chopped
- ¼ cup fresh parsley, chopped
- Salt and pepper
- 2 eggs, lightly beaten
- ½ cup ricotta cheese
- 1 tablespoon ground coriander
- 1 tablespoon fresh oregano
- 1 cup crumbled feta cheese
- 8 sheets phyllo dough
- ¼ cup olive oil

1. Preheat the oven to 350 degrees Fahrenheit. Lightly oil a 9- by 9-inch baking pan.

2. Heat the olive oil in a large skillet over medium heat.

3. Sauté the onion and garlic until soft and lightly browned.

4. Stir in the spinach and parsley. Continue to sauté until the spinach is limp, about 2 minutes. Season with salt and pepper. Remove from heat, and set aside to cool.

5. In a medium bowl, mix together the eggs, ricotta, coriander, oregano, and feta. Stir in the spinach mixture.

6. Lay 1 sheet of phyllo dough in the baking pan and brush it lightly with olive oil. (Be sure to cover the dough you're not using with a damp cloth or it will dry out.)

7. Lay a second sheet of phyllo dough on top, brush it with olive oil, and repeat the process with 2 more sheets of phyllo. The sheets will overlap the pan.

8. Spread the spinach and cheese mixture into the pan, and fold the overhanging dough over the filling. Brush the top with oil.

9. Layer the remaining 4 sheets of phyllo dough, brushing each with oil. Tuck overhanging dough into the pan to seal the filling.

10. Bake the spanakopita for 30 to 40 minutes, until golden brown. Cut it into squares and serve it while it's hot.

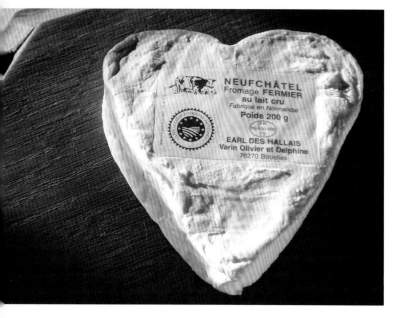

Neufchâtel

Like many other French cheeses, Neufchâtel bears the name of its village of origin in Normandy. It can be eaten fresh or molded into the familiar heart-shaped pattern and aged until it develops a white rind. Because it's enriched with cream, Neufchâtel is about 45 percent butterfat. To enhance its flavor before you serve it, add crushed pineapple or chives, garlic, scallions, and olives.

Yield: 1½ to 2 pounds

Ingredients:

- ❧ 1 gallon pasteurized whole milk
- ❧ 1 pint pasteurized heavy cream
- ❧ ¼ teaspoon direct-set mesophilic culture or 4 tablespoons mesophilic mother culture
- ❧ 3 drops liquid rennet, diluted in ⅓ cup cool unchlorinated water
- ❧ Kosher salt

1. In a double boiler or water bath, combine the milk and cream. Heat the mixture to 80 degrees Fahrenheit.

2. Add the culture, let it dissolve in milk for 2 minutes, and mix well.

3. Add 1 teaspoon of the diluted rennet and stir gently, top to bottom.

4. Cover the milk and let stand at room temperature (at least 72 degrees Fahrenheit) for 12 hours or until a thick curd has formed.

5. Carefully pour off the surface whey. Spoon the curd into a colander lined with butter muslin with a catch bowl beneath.

6. Tie the ends of the muslin into a knot, and hang the bag to drain until it has stopped dripping whey. This may take 10 to 12 hours.

7. Place the bag(s) back into your colander, and place the colander in a pot. Put a plate on the bag and a weight on the plate (1 to 2 pounds, or a full liquid-quart container, is enough).

8. Cover the pot and refrigerate for 12 hours.

9. Remove the cheese from the bag, and mix in Kosher salt and any herbs to taste.

10. Shape into patties, wrap them separately in wax paper, and store them for up to 2 weeks.

Variation: Aged Neufchâtel

Wait until you've mastered fresh cheeses before you try this recipe. You will need several Camembert molds and a ripening container.

Yield: 1½ to 2 pounds

Ingredients:

❖ See ingredients for Neufchâtel

❖ 1 pinch *Penicillium candidum*

1. Follow steps 1 through 8 in the recipe for Neufchâtel. However, in step 2, add the *P. candidum* along with the culture. Mix well.

2. Remove the curd, mix in salt to taste, and place the cheese into molds in a ripening container.

3. Refrigerate the cheese for 1 day; wipe away any collected whey.

4. When the cheese is firm, take it out of the molds. Place the cheese on mats in a clean ripening container. Ripen for 7 to 10 days at 50 degrees Fahrenheit and 90 percent humidity. Turn the cheese over daily, and remove any moisture from the container. You should begin to see a white mold bloom on the rind after 1 week.

5. When the cheese is covered with white mold, wrap it in cheese wrap or wax paper (not plastic wrap). Continue to ripen the cheese until it feels soft when pressed at the center. Once ripened to taste, store it in the refrigerator. The white mold is edible, but you can trim it away if desired.

See the next page for a cheesecake recipe that uses Neufchâtel.

Neufchâtel Cheesecake

Substitute Neufchâtel for cream cheese in any of your favorite recipes, such as this one. Folding in the beaten egg whites keeps this cake light, moist, and luscious.

Yield: 10 servings

Ingredients:

Cheesecake

* 4 eggs
* 1 cup sugar
* 2 tablespoons flour
* ¼ teaspoon salt
* 1 pound Neufchâtel
* ½ teaspoon vanilla

Crust

* 1 cup crushed graham crackers
* ¼ cup melted butter
* ¼ teaspoon cinnamon
* ¼ teaspoon nutmeg

Topping

* 1 cup homemade sour cream (see page 59 for the recipe)
* 1 teaspoon vanilla
* 2 tablespoons sugar
* Ground cinnamon

1. Set the oven to 375 degrees Fahrenheit.
2. Make the crust by combining all crust ingredients in a large bowl. Butter a 9-inch springform pan, and press the mixture into its bottom and up about 1 inch on all sides. Bake for 5 minutes or until the crust is set.
3. To prepare the cheesecake filling, first separate the eggs.
4. Beat the egg whites with ¼ cup sugar until stiff. Set aside.
5. In a large mixing bowl, beat the egg yolks until thick. Beat in ¾ cup sugar, flour, vanilla, and salt.
6. Stir in the cheese, bit by bit.
7. Fold in the egg whites.
8. Pour the cheesecake mixture into the crust. Bake at 375 degrees for about 20 to 30 minutes or until firm to the touch.
9. To make the topping, mix all topping ingredients together. When the cheesecake is cool, smooth the topping onto its surface.
10. Bake the cake for 5 more minutes at 400 degrees Fahrenheit, taking care not to burn the cream topping.
11. Cool, add fruit if desired, and then chill.

Cream Cheese

The first American version of an old Norman recipe for cream cheese was branded "Philadelphia" in 1880. But the taste of homemade cream cheese trumps anything store-bought because it eliminates additives such as gum and stabilizers.

Yield: 1 pound

Ingredients:

❖ 2 quarts pasteurized half-and-half creamer

❖ ¼ teaspoon direct-set mesophilic culture or 4 tablespoons mesophilic mother culture

❖ Kosher salt

1. Bring the half-and-half to room temperature. If it's too cold, place it in a water bath. Check that the temperature is at least 72 degrees Fahrenheit.

2. Add the culture and let it dissolve in the milk for 2 minutes. Mix well, top to bottom.

3. Cover and let stand for 12 hours or until a firm curd has formed.

4. Check coagulation by tipping the bowl. If there's still movement, give it more time. The cheese has set when it has a firm, yogurtlike consistency.

5. Pour the mixture into a butter muslin-lined colander with a catch bowl beneath.

6. Tie the ends of the muslin, and let the cheese ball drain.

7. When it stops dripping, put the cheese in a bowl and add salt to taste.

8. Place the cheese into small molds, and refrigerate for 4 to 6 hours to firm.

9. Wrap the finished cheeses individually. They will keep for up to 2 weeks.

Orange Cream Cheese Pound Cake

Yield: 10 to 12 servings

Ingredients:

❖ 1 cup butter, softened (see page 58 for a recipe)

❖ 1 cup homemade cream cheese, softened

❖ 2 cups sugar

❖ 1 teaspoon salt

❖ 6 eggs, at room temperature

❖ ¼ cup frozen orange juice concentrate, thawed

❖ 1 tablespoon vanilla

❖ 3 cups unbleached all-purpose flour, sifted

1. Preheat oven to 325 degrees Fahrenheit.

2. Butter and flour a 12-cup Bundt pan.

3. Beat the butter and cream cheese in a large bowl using an electric mixer until fluffy, about 3 minutes.

4. Add the sugar and salt, and beat another 3 minutes.

5. Add the eggs, one at a time, beating well.

6. Beat in the orange juice concentrate and vanilla.

7. Beat in the flour at low speed until the batter is smooth.

8. Pour the batter into the pan and bake for 1 hour or until a toothpick inserted at the center comes out clean.

9. Cool the cake in its pan for 15 minutes, then turn it out on a rack.

Crème Fraîche

This French cultured cream gets thicker and more tart as it matures. Drained, it becomes mascarpone. Crème fraîche is a creative chef's best friend. Add it to sauces served with fish, poultry, and vegetables; to soup for creamy richness; and to fruit as a topping. For desserts, you may want to whip and sweeten the crème fraîche with honey and a bit of vanilla extract.

Yield: 1 quart

Ingredients:

❧ 1 quart pasteurized heavy cream

❧ ¼ teaspoon Flora Danica (mesophilic aromatic culture)

1. Warm the cream to 80 degrees Fahrenheit using a bowl of hot water.

2. Add the culture and let it dissolve for 2 minutes. Stir well, top to bottom. Cover the cream and let it ripen at room temperature (72 degrees Fahrenheit) for 12 to 24 hours or until the cream is very thick.

3. Use immediately, or spoon it into an airtight container; it will keep refrigerated for several weeks.

Variation: Mascarpone

Mascarpone is used in the regional dishes of Lombardy and in desserts such as cannoli and tiramisu. Here are two different recipes—one using culture as a starter; another using tartaric acid, which is derived from tamarind seed.

WITH CULTURE

Yield: 2 cups

Ingredients:

❖ 1 quart pasteurized heavy cream

❖ ¼ teaspoon Flora Danica (mesophilic aromatic culture)

1. Follow the steps for making crème fraîche.
2. Ladle the coagulated curd into a colander lined with muslin.
3. Drain the curd in the refrigerator for 1 to 4 hours or until it reaches the consistency you want.
4. Remove the mascarpone from the colander, and spoon it into an airtight container. It will keep refrigerated for several weeks.

WITH TARTARIC ACID

Yield: 2 cups

Ingredients:

❖ 1 quart heavy cream

❖ ¼ teaspoon tartaric acid

1. Pour the cream into the inner pot of a double boiler; fill the outer pot with cold water. Heat the cream to 190 degrees Fahrenheit, stirring gently. Remove from heat.
2. Add the tartaric acid and stir for several minutes. The mixture will curdle and thicken.
3. Line a colander with a double layer of muslin and ladle in the curd.
4. Drain for 1 hour or until it reaches the consistency you want.
5. Cover and store the mascarpone in the refrigerator for up to 4 days.

Tiramisu

Sugar, chocolate, and espresso? No wonder Italians call this caffeinated, layered cake a "pick me up." The inclusion of zabaglione custard is a Venetian specialty.

Yield: 12 servings

Ingredients:

Cream

- 6 extra-large egg yolks, brought to room temperature
- ½ cup granulated sugar
- ¾ cup milk
- 1 pound mascarpone cheese

Cake

- 8 ounces bittersweet chocolate
- 24 crisp Italian ladyfingers
- 2 cups heavy cream
- 1 tablespoon granulated sugar
- 1 teaspoon confectioners' sugar
- 2 cups strong espresso coffee, cooled

PREPARING THE CREAM

1. Bring water to a boil in the outer pan of a double boiler.
2. In a glass bowl, combine the egg yolks and sugar; stir until the sugar is completely dissolved and the egg yolks turn a lighter color.
3. Add the milk and mix thoroughly. Transfer the mixture to the inner pot of the double boiler.
4. Stir constantly in the same direction until the cream is thick enough to coat the spoon—just before it's about to boil. Do not allow the mixture to boil.
5. Remove the cream from heat, and continue to stir for 1 minute longer. Then transfer the cream to a glass bowl to cool, about 1 hour.
6. Place the mascarpone in the bowl of a food processor, add the cooled cream, and blend well until a very smooth and light cream forms. Do not overbeat, as the mascarpone will separate. Refrigerate until needed.

LAYERING THE TIRAMISU

1. Coarsely grate or shave the chocolate.
2. Place the ladyfingers in one layer on a jelly-roll pan or rimmed cookie sheet.

3. Whip the heavy cream, granulated sugar, and confectioners' sugar in a chilled metal bowl using a wire whisk.

4. Add the cooled cream/mascarpone mixture and whisk very well.

5. Soak the ladyfingers in the cold coffee, and gently transfer 12 of them to a 14-inch trifle dish or similar glass bowl.

6. Spread half of the cream on top of the ladyfingers; then sprinkle half of the chocolate on top of that.

7. Make one more layer using the remaining ingredients; then cover the whole thing with plastic wrap. Refrigerate for at least 1 hour before serving.

Whey Ricotta

Traditionally, ricotta was a by-product of sheep's milk cheese. Because sheep's milk is hard to come by, this recipe uses whey drained from cow's milk cheese instead. In Italian, ricotta means "recooked." Today, we might call the cheese "recycled." If you want to use fresh whey, have these ingredients at hand while you're making hard cheese.

Yield: about 1 cup

Ingredients:

❖ 2 gallons fresh whey, no more than 3 hours old

❖ 1 quart whole milk, to increase the yield (optional)

❖ ¼ cup cider vinegar

❖ 4 ounces mesophilic mother culture, to enhance flavor (optional)

❖ Kosher salt (optional)

1. Pour the whey into a large pot. Add the milk, if desired, and heat to 200 degrees Fahrenheit. Stir to prevent scorching, and do not boil.

2. Turn the heat off, add the vinegar, and stir. You will see tiny curd particles on the surface.

3. Gently ladle the curds into a muslin-lined colander. Allow to drain into a catch bowl.

4. If desired, now is the time to fold in the mesophilic starter.

5. When the curds are cool to the touch, tie the corners of the muslin into a knot and hang the bag over your sink to drain.

6. Let the cheese drain for 1 hour for soft ricotta or several hours for firm.

7. Put the cheese in a bowl. Add salt and herbs to taste, if desired. The ricotta will keep refrigerated for 1 week.

Dill Bread

You can substitute water for whey in this recipe and small-curd cottage cheese for ricotta, if you don't have either on hand.

Yield: 2 small loaves

Ingredients:

- ½ cup whey
- 1 tablespoon yeast
- 2 tablespoons butter
- 2 cups ricotta
- 3 tablespoons sugar (or another sweetener)
- 1 small onion, minced
- 2 teaspoons dill weed
- 2 teaspoons dill seed
- 1½ teaspoons salt
- ½ teaspoon baking soda
- ½ cup wheat germ
- 4 to 5 cups flour

1. Heat the whey until it is lukewarm, place it in a large mixing bowl, and mix in the yeast.
2. In a pan, melt the butter and stir in the ricotta.
3. To the yeast mixture, add the sugar, onion, dill weed and seed, salt, and baking soda. Blend well.
4. Add the wheat germ and the ricotta mixture to the yeast mixture. Blend well.
5. Add 1½ cups of flour and mix well. (If you're using a heavy-duty mixer, beat at medium speed for 5 minutes.)
6. Slowly add the remaining flour until the dough holds together and isn't sticky.
7. Turn the dough out onto a floured board, and knead until the dough springs back when you poke it with your finger.
8. Put the dough in a greased bowl, cover, and let rise until it has doubled in size.
9. Punch the dough down, knead it briefly, and divide it in half.
10. Shape the dough into loaves and place them in greased bread pans. Cover and let rise until the dough has doubled in size.
11. Bake the loaves in a preheated oven at 350 degrees Fahrenheit for about 50 minutes. The bread is done when it shrinks from the sides of the pan. Also, the bottom will sound hollow when you tap it.
12. Turn the loaves out of their pans and onto a wire rack to cool.

Gjetost and Mysost

Another use for leftover whey is to make these popular Scandinavian cheeses. Gjetost (pronounced YET-ohst) is made with goat's milk whey; mysost (pronounced ME-sohst) is made with cow's milk whey. Cheese color ranges from tan to dark brown depending on sugar caramelization. Both take hours of boiling, so plan accordingly.

Yield: 1½ pounds

Ingredients:

❖ 1 gallon fresh whey, no more than 3 hours old

❖ 1 cup heavy cream (optional)

1. Pour the whey into a pot and bring to a boil. Skim off the foam using a slotted spoon and reserve in the refrigerator.

2. Turn down the heat to a simmer, and let the whey boil uncovered over low heat until it's reduced to three quarters of its original volume. Stir often to prevent sticking. (This may take up to 12 hours.)

3. Add the reserved foam, and stir as the whey thickens.

4. Add cream, if desired. The amount will determine the cheese's final consistency.

5. When the cheese has the consistency of fudge, put your pot into a sink of cold water (a water bath). Careful: it will be very hot. Keep stirring.

6. When the cheese starts to firm up, place it in airtight containers and refrigerate it. These cheeses will keep refrigerated for up to 1 month.

CHAPTER 6

Stretched Curds

Stretched-curd cheese is the next logical step for a novice cheese maker because it requires no pressing or aging. These cheeses, including mozzarella, can be eaten right away. Their famous elasticity and melting qualities are a result of heating the cut curd in very hot water, then kneading and shaping it. Finally, it's plunged into ice water to firm it up. Because of the high temperature required, you will add thermophilic (heat-loving) culture rather than mesophilic culture to your milk.

THE BRINE BATH

Some cheeses in this section are soaked in a heavily salted solution called a brine bath. The first time you make it, use the following preparation:

> "A poet's hope:
> to be, like some
> valley cheese,
> local, but prized
> elsewhere."
> —W. H. Auden

1. Heat 1 gallon of water to 190 degrees Fahrenheit (nearly boiling); add 1 tablespoon of calcium chloride per gallon of water.
2. Dissolve 2 pounds of Kosher salt in the water.
3. Chill before using.

To reuse your brine, boil it, add salt until it no longer dissolves, let it cool, and refrigerate it. Make sure the container you choose is noncorrosive (glass or stainless steel).

EQUIPMENT

To make stretched-curd cheeses, you will need a pair of heat-resistant rubber gloves or two wooden spoons, a bowl of ice water, and enough Kosher salt for the brine. If you have a pH meter, now is your chance to use it to test acidity (the target acidity for stretching is 5.2). Finally, if you want to age provolone, you will need an ambient temperature of 62 to 65 degrees Fahrenheit and 80 to 85 percent humidity. If you don't have a "cold room" or cheese cave, save this recipe until you do.

Stretched-Curd Cheese Recipes

When recipes call for it, be sure to increase the heat by no more than 2 degrees every 5 minutes.

Traditional Mozzarella

Americans' love of pizza means we eat tons of mozzarella. But if you've only had low-moisture "pizza cheese," you'll be surprised to learn that fresh mozzarella should never be rubbery or hard. It should be so soft that it weeps its own milky whey when cut.

In Italy, the sweetest, richest mozzarella is made with the milk of a water buffalo (*mozzarella di bufala*). Water buffalo have grazed the hills south and west of Naples since the second century AD. Today, Italians buy as much *mozzarella di latte* (from cow's milk) as *mozzarella di bufala* because it's half as expensive. They also relish *Bocconcini*, small balls of mozzarella that are marinated and served as appetizers.

Brine for a brine bath.

Whether you choose this recipe or the short-cut version that follows may depend on how much time you have and how much yield you need. The longer traditional method gets its acidity from thermophilic culture, which takes time to ripen the milk. The shorter method uses citric acid, which is faster but yields less cheese for the same amount of milk.

Yield: about 2 pounds

Ingredients:

❖ 2 gallons nonhomogenized whole milk

❖ ¼ teaspoon direct-set thermophilic culture or 4 tablespoons thermophilic mother culture

❖ ¼ teaspoon lipase powder, diluted in ¼ cup cool water and allowed to sit 20 minutes (optional, for stronger flavor)

❖ ½ teaspoon liquid rennet, diluted in ¼ cup cool unchlorinated water

❖ Brine bath (see page 76)

1. In a double boiler or water bath, warm the milk to 90 degrees Fahrenheit, stirring gently.

2. Add the culture and let it dissolve on the milk's surface for 2 minutes. Blend well using an up-and-down motion. Mix in the lipase, if desired. Cover and let ripen for 45 minutes.

3. Add the diluted rennet and mix well from top to bottom using a skimmer. Cover and let set at 90 degrees Fahrenheit for 1 hour or until you get a clean break. Curd is ready when it separates cleanly and whey fills the cut.

4. Gently cut the curd into ½-inch cubes, vertically and horizontally, in a grid pattern. Let the curd settle for 5 minutes.

5. Gradually warm the curd to 102 degrees Fahrenheit, stirring gently. Raise the temperature no more than 2 degrees Fahrenheit every 5 minutes. This will take about 30 minutes. Once the curd reaches 102 degrees Fahrenheit, let it sit for 5 minutes.

6. Drain off the whey through a muslin-lined colander, and reserve it for making ricotta (see recipe on page 73). Cover the curd in the now-empty pot, and hold it at 102 degrees Fahrenheit for up to 2½ hours. Occasionally drain off any whey, and turn the curd mass over as it acidifies.

7. In a separate pot, bring 2 quarts of water to 175 degrees Fahrenheit.

8. Test the curd for readiness after 2 hours. If you are using a pH meter, you can begin stretching the curd when it reaches 5.2 on the scale. If you aren't using a meter, test the curd's "stretchability" by immersing a small piece in 175 degrees Fahrenheit water and working it with your gloved fingers or with two wooden spoons. If it's ready, the surface will shine, and it will stretch like taffy. If it's not ready, let the curd rest for a few minutes and test again.

9. When it's ready, remove the curd from the pot, and place it on a draining board. Cut it into ½-inch cubes. Put the cubes in a stainless-steel bowl and pour water (heated to 175 degrees Fahrenheit) over them.

10. Using spoons or wearing gloves, scoop up some of the curd and knead and shape it into a ball. Lift the ball and stretch it into a rope. Fold the rope back on itself, and pull it out again. When the surface is smooth and shiny, shape it into a ball or braid it (your choice). If the curd breaks instead of stretching, it's too cool; dip it in the hot water to warm it up.

11. Place the cheese into a bowl of ice water to firm it up. When it's chilled, soak it in a brine bath for 2 to 3 hours, turning it over several times. Eat the mozzarella fresh, or store it refrigerated in brine for up to a week.

Grating Tip

To grate mozzarella, freeze it first. Wrap your fresh mozzarella in plastic wrap and freeze it for at least 15 minutes. Unwrap the cheese and then grate it.

Variation: Short-Cut Mozzarella

This recipe eliminates the brine bath and speeds milk acidification by substituting citric acid for thermophilic culture. (You can also use white vinegar.) Most beginners find that they need to make more than one batch of mozzarella in order to practice stretching the curd. If you choose to do that, reduce the amounts for the ingredients by half.

Yield: about 1½ pounds

Ingredients:

❖ 2 gallons nonhomogenized whole milk

❖ 1½ teaspoons citric acid powder dissolved in ½ cup cool water

❖ ¼ teaspoon lipase powder, diluted in ¼ cup cool water and allowed to sit 20 minutes (optional, for stronger flavor)

❖ ¼ teaspoon liquid rennet, diluted in ¼ cup cool unchlorinated water

❖ ¼ cup Kosher salt

1. Combine the milk and citric acid, stirring well from top to bottom. Blend in the lipase, if desired.

2. In a double boiler or water bath, warm the milk to 88 degrees Fahrenheit, stirring gently.

3. Add the diluted rennet and mix well from top to bottom using a skimmer. Cover and let set at 88 degrees Fahrenheit for 30 minutes or until you get a clean break.

4. Gently cut the curd into ½-inch cubes, vertically and horizontally, in a grid pattern. Let the curd settle for 5 minutes.

5. Gradually warm the curd to 106 degrees Fahrenheit, stirring gently. This will take about 20 minutes. Once the curd reaches 106 degrees Fahrenheit, stir for 20 more minutes, and let sit for 5 minutes. Meanwhile, in another pot, bring 2 quarts of water to 175 degrees Fahrenheit. Add salt and stir until dissolved.

6. Ladle the curd into a muslin-lined colander. Let it drain for 10 minutes, but keep it warm. You can use the leftover whey in breads or soups but not for ricotta (the citric acid in this recipe makes the whey too acidic for ricotta).

7. Place the block of curd on a draining board, and cut it into ½-inch cubes. Put the cubes in a stainless-steel bowl and pour the hot salted water over them. The cheese needs to be nearly melting (145 degrees Fahrenheit) to stretch.

8. Wearing heat-resistant rubber gloves or using wooden spoons, scoop up some of the curd under the water and shape it into a ball. Lift the ball and stretch it into a rope. Fold the rope back on itself, and pull it out again. When the surface is smooth and glossy, shape it into a ball or braid it (your choice). If the curd breaks instead of stretching, it's too cool; dip it in the hot water to warm it.

9. Place the cheese into a bowl of ice water to firm it up. When it's firm, remove it and drain it on paper towel. Eat it fresh, or wrap and refrigerate it.

King of Naples Salad

This is a memorable way to showcase your fresh mozzarella, especially if you're of Italian heritage. Red (tomato), white (cheese), and green (avocado) represent the colors of Italy's flag. I like a simple dressing of extra virgin olive oil and balsamic vinegar; you can substitute your own favorite dressing.

Yield: 4 servings

Ingredients:

❧ 1 large ripe avocado, peeled and sliced ¼-inch thick

❧ 1 large ripe tomato, peeled and sliced ¼-inch thick

❧ 8 ounces fresh mozzarella, sliced ¼-inch thick

❧ Salt

❧ Freshly ground pepper

❧ Extra virgin olive oil

❧ Balsamic vinegar

❧ 8 leaves fresh basil

1. Brush the avocado slices with lemon juice so they won't darken. Arrange them in an overlapping column on the left side of a platter.

2. Arrange the tomato slices in an overlapping column on the right side of a platter.

3. Place the mozzarella slices in a column down the middle.

4. Sprinkle all with salt and pepper to taste, then drizzle them with oil and vinegar, also to taste. Garnish with the fresh basil.

Polenta Pizza

An alternative to pastry-dough pizza, this one boasts a thick and crunchy cornmeal crust.

Yield: 4 to 5 servings

Ingredients:

Filling

- 1 tablespoon olive oil
- 1 small onion, thinly sliced
- ½ cup thinly sliced bell pepper
- 10 mushrooms, sliced
- 1 small zucchini, thinly sliced
- 5 to 6 medium cloves garlic, crushed
- 2 teaspoons fresh basil, minced
- ½ teaspoon dried oregano
- Freshly ground black pepper
- ¼ pound mozzarella, shredded
- 1 medium-size ripe tomato, sliced

Polenta Crust

- 2 cups water
- 1½ cups coarse cornmeal
- 1 teaspoon salt
- 1½ cups cold water
- 1 tablespoon olive oil

1. Bring 2 cups water to a boil in a saucepan.

2. Combine the cornmeal, salt, and cold water in a small bowl. Whisk it into the boiling water.

3. Cook the polenta for about 10 minutes over low heat, stirring frequently. It will get very thick. Remove from heat, and let cool.

4. Preheat the oven to 375 degrees Fahrenheit. Oil a 10-inch pie pan. Add the polenta, and use a spoon and/or your wet hands to form it into a smooth, thick crust over the bottom and sides of the pan. Brush the surface with olive oil, and bake uncovered for 45 minutes.

5. While the crust bakes, heat 1 tablespoon of olive oil in a medium-size skillet. Add the onion and sauté it for 5 minutes or until it begins to soften. Add the bell pepper, mushrooms, and zucchini, and sauté until everything is tender. Stir in the garlic, herbs, and some black pepper. Do not overcook.

6. Remove the pie pan from the oven and set aside. Raise the oven temperature to "Broil." Sprinkle half of the cheese onto the bottom of the baked crust. Add the tomato slices. Spread the sautéed veggies over the tomatoes, and sprinkle the remaining cheese on top. Broil until brown (about 5 minutes) and serve hot.

Scamorza

In Italy, scamorza is sold plain or smoked in 8-ounce fern-wrapped balls. Most Italian scamorza comes from Lombardy, where carving animals from the cheese is a tradition. Depending on the season, you might see spring lambs, Christmas donkeys, pigs, whales, ducks, and owls. Instead of carving the finished cheese, try twisting the warm curd into unusual shapes.

Yield: 1½ pounds

Ingredients:

❖ 2 gallons nonhomogenized whole milk

❖ ¼ teaspoon direct-set thermophilic culture or 4 tablespoons thermophilic mother culture

❖ ¼ teaspoon liquid rennet, diluted in ¼ cup cool unchlorinated water

❖ Brine bath (see page 76)

1. In a double boiler or water bath, warm the milk to 96 degrees Fahrenheit, stirring gently.

2. Add the culture and let it dissolve on the milk's surface for 2 minutes. Stir from top to bottom until well mixed. Cover and let ripen for 45 minutes.

3. Add the diluted rennet and mix well from top to bottom using a skimmer. Cover and let set at 96 degrees Fahrenheit for 1 hour or until you get a clean break.

4. Gently cut the curd into ½-inch cubes, vertically and horizontally, in a grid pattern. Let the curd settle for 5 minutes.

5. Gradually warm the curd to 104 degrees Fahrenheit, stirring gently, for no less than 30 minutes. Do not heat too quickly. Once the target temperature is reached, stir for another 15 minutes. Let the curd settle, then pour off the whey and return the curd to the empty pot. Replace the cover and let the curd acidify. Turn it over to help the drainage, and remove any whey.

6. In a separate pot, bring 2 quarts of water to 175 degrees Fahrenheit.

7. Test the curd for readiness after 2 hours. If you are using a pH meter, the curd is ready to be stretched when it reaches 5.2. If you aren't using a meter, begin testing the curd's "stretchability" by immersing a small piece in water at 175 degrees Fahrenheit and working it with your gloved fingers or with two wooden spoons. If it's ready, the surface will shine, and it will stretch like taffy.

8. When it's ready, remove the curd from the pot, and place it on a draining board. Cut it into ½-inch cubes; place the cubes in a stainless-steel bowl, and pour the water (that's been heated to 175 degrees Fahrenheit) over them.

9. Knead and shape the curd under the water into a firm ball. Lift the ball and stretch it into a rope. Fold the rope back on itself, and pull it out again. If the curd breaks instead of stretching, it's too cool; immerse it in the hot water until it becomes elastic. You can shape your cheese any way you want to.

10. When the cheese is smooth and shiny, place it into a bowl of ice water to firm it up.

11. Place the chilled cheese in a brine bath at room temperature. A 2-pound piece of cheese will need 12 hours, smaller cheeses will require just a few hours. Halfway through, turn the cheese over once.

12. Air-dry the cheese on a rack at room temperature for 1 to 2 days or until it's dry to the touch. Eat it fresh, or refrigerate it for up to 2 weeks.

Asadero

One of many Mexican cheeses popular on the West Coast for its great melting quality, asadero is great for nachos, quesadillas, and enchiladas. *Asadero* means "roastable" in Spanish.

Yield: about 2 pounds

Ingredients:

❖ 2 gallons nonhomogenized whole milk

❖ ¼ teaspoon direct-set thermophilic culture or 4 tablespoons thermophilic mother culture

❖ ¼ teaspoon liquid rennet, diluted in ¼ cup cool unchlorinated water

❖ Brine bath (see page 76)

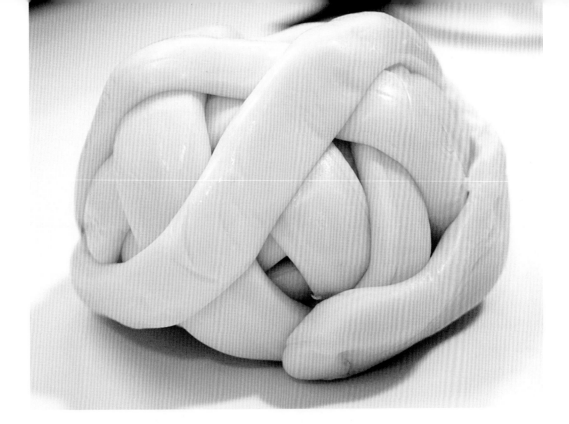

1. In a double boiler or water bath, warm the milk to 99 degrees Fahrenheit, stirring gently.

2. Add the culture and let it dissolve on the milk's surface for 2 minutes. Stir from top to bottom until well mixed. Cover and let ripen for 45 minutes.

3. Add the diluted rennet and mix well from top to bottom using a skimmer. Cover and let set at 99 degrees Fahrenheit for 45 minutes or until you get a clean break.

4. Gently cut the curd into ½-inch cubes, vertically and horizontally, in a grid pattern. Let it settle for s5 minutes. Stir for 30 minutes, and then let it settle again.

5. With a measuring cup, remove a third of the whey, and replace it with the same amount of water heated to 125 degrees Fahrenheit to bring the temperature of the curd to 108 degrees Fahrenheit.

6. Stir the curd for 30 minutes, and then let it settle at 108 degrees Fahrenheit for 1 hour. While the curd acidifies, heat 2 quarts of water to 175 degrees Fahrenheit.

7. Pour the curd into a cloth-lined colander, and reserve the whey for other recipes. Let the curd drain until it holds together.

8. Place the curd on a draining board and cut it into 2-inch cubes. Place the pieces in a stainless-steel bowl and pour the hot water over them.

9. Wearing heat-resistant rubber gloves, work the curd under the water into a firm ball. Place the ball on your cutting board and knead it until it's shiny and smooth. If the curd cools and becomes stiff, immerse it in hot water until it becomes elastic again.

10. Place your cheese into a bowl of ice water to firm it up. After about 15 minutes in the ice water, let the cheese soak in a brine bath for 30 minutes. Air-dry the cheese on a rack.

11. Eat it fresh, or refrigerate it for up to 2 weeks.

Provolone

Like all *pasta filata* (Italian for "stretched curd") cheeses, provolone lends itself to improvisation. You'll find it shaped like torpedoes, gourds, salamis, and balls—always rope-bound. Its namesake is based on Provola, a Southern Italian cheese, and its cousin, *Caciocavallo*, which means "cheese on horseback" because it was cured on a rope straddling a high beam, similar to how a person rides *a cavallo*, "on horseback." Imported provolone is sold *dolce* (mild) or *piccante* (sharp). Add zing to your next omelet by sprinkling on some sharp provolone.

Yield: 1 pound

Ingredients:

❖ 1 gallon nonhomogenized whole or partially skimmed milk

❖ ¼ teaspoon direct-set thermophilic culture or 4 tablespoons thermophilic mother culture

❖ ¼ teaspoon lipase powder, diluted in ¼ cup cool water and allowed to sit 20 minutes (optional, for stronger flavor)

❖ ¼ teaspoon liquid rennet, diluted in ¼ cup cool unchlorinated water

❖ Brine bath (see page 76)

1. In a double boiler or water bath, warm the milk to 96 degrees Fahrenheit, stirring gently.

2. Add the culture and let it dissolve on the milk's surface for 2 minutes. Stir from top to bottom until it's well mixed. Cover and let ripen for 1 hour.

3. Add the lipase, stir, and let rest for 10 minutes.

4. Add the diluted rennet and mix well from top to bottom using a skimmer. Cover and let set at 96 degrees Fahrenheit for 30 minutes or until you get a clean break.

5. Gently cut the curd into ½-inch cubes, vertically and horizontally, in a grid pattern. Let the curd settle for 5 minutes.

6. Gradually heat the curd to 145 degrees Fahrenheit, stirring gently, over a period of 1 hour. Do not heat too quickly. Let the curd settle for 10 minutes.

7. Ladle the curd into a muslin-lined colander, place the colander over the whey pot, and cover it to keep it warm.

8. While the curd is draining, heat 2 quarts of water to 175 degrees Fahrenheit.

9. If you are using a pH meter, the curd is ready to be stretched when it reaches 5.2. If you aren't using a meter, begin testing the curd's "stretchability" by immersing a small piece in 175 degrees Fahrenheit water and working it with your gloved fingers or with two wooden spoons. If it's ready, the surface will shine, and it will stretch like taffy.

10. Place the curd on a draining board, and cut it into 1-inch cubes. Put the pieces in a stainless-steel bowl and pour the water (heated to 175 degrees Fahrenheit) over them.

11. Wearing gloves or using spoons, knead the curd under the water to release whey. Work it into a firm ball. Lift the ball and stretch it into a rope. Fold the rope back on itself, and pull it out again. Repeat pulling and folding until the cheese is smooth and shiny. If the curd cools and becomes stiff, immerse it in the hot water until it becomes elastic again. Finally, shape a top-knot on the ball so that you can hang it.

12. Place the cheese into a bowl of ice water to firm it up, and then put it in the brine. Let it soak in the brine at room temperature for about 3 hours, turning it over once.

13. Pat the cheese dry and tie it with a cord. Hang the cheese for 3 weeks at 50 degrees Fahrenheit, or let it ripen in a plastic container at the same temperature. Turn the cheese daily for the first 2 weeks, then twice in the last week. If mold appears, wipe it off using a vinegar-salt solution (1 teaspoon Kosher salt to ¼ cup vinegar).

14. For sharper flavor, continue aging the cheese at 62 to 65 degrees Fahrenheit and 80 to 85 percent humidity. After 1 month, rub the cheese with olive oil. Repeat this once a month to encourage a natural rind. Cure the provolone for 4 months for table cheese or for 6 to 12 months for grating cheese.

CHAPTER 7

Semi-Hard Cheese

Unlike fresh (bag) cheeses that require little equipment and no aging, cheese recipes in this and all following chapters require more time and equipment. They also require a bit of delayed gratification; you'll need to wait a few months, rather than a few hours, to sample the miracle of your wizardry.

> "Age is something that doesn't matter unless you are a cheese."
>
> —Helen Hayes

The wait is worth it. You'll appreciate the complexity of an aged cheese's flavor and texture compared to that of fresh cheeses. These are the next step in mastering techniques refined over centuries. Our equipment and ingredients may be modern, but the principles of artisan cheese making resist shortcuts.

So, what does semi-hard mean? A cheese's moisture content determines its consistency. While fresh cheese retains high moisture, semi-hard cheese has 40 to 50 percent moisture.

PRESSING AND AGING SEMI-HARD CHEESE

Before you start making recipes in this chapter, review the information in chapter 3 regarding the following techniques:

- ♣ Salting curds
- ♣ Pressing curds
- ♣ Bandaging
- ♣ Aging
- ♣ Molding curds
- ♣ Air-drying
- ♣ Waxing
- ♣ Testing acidity

Most cheese is air-dried to form a protective rind before it's aged. Then it can cure with a natural rind or be wrapped in muslin and coated with vegetable shortening to prevent moisture loss through evaporation. Another way to seal in moisture and slow mold growth is to wax your cheese. Edam is famous for its red wax, Cheddar for its cloth bandage. In both cases, an edible rind forms beneath the covering. The advantage of a cloth covering over a wax one is that the cheese can breathe but still retains moisture.

The purpose of waxing and bandaging is to protect the cheese as it ages. Maintaining proper temperature and humidity allows the cheese to develop its full flavor and texture; the longer it ages, the stronger its flavor. Most semi-hard cheeses ripen best at 50 to 55 degrees Fahrenheit and 80 to 85 percent humidity.

Waxing Cheddar cheese.

EQUIPMENT

More advanced cheese making requires more advanced tools, all of which are available from suppliers (see Resources, page 173). A serious cheese maker will want a cheese press with a pressure gauge and a dedicated refrigerator or wine cooler that allows climate control. Improvisation is fine while you're experimenting with recipes, but proper equipment saves time. In addition to the basic tools, to make semi-hard cheeses, you will also need:

❖ A cheese press
❖ Cheese boards
❖ pH testing equipment
❖ A ripening cave (usually a dedicated refrigerator)
❖ A thermometer/hygrometer (to measure temperature and relative humidity)
❖ A 2-pound tomme or other large mold
❖ Cheese wax or muslin for bandaging
❖ Drying mats (plastic or bamboo sushi mats)

Gouda ripening on a bamboo mat in a cheese cave.

Semi-Hard Cheese Recipes

For all semi-hard cheese, increase the heat when recipes call for it by no more than 2 degrees every 5 minutes.

Traditional Cheddar

Cheddar originated in the late 1500s in an English village by the same name. By the 1800s, most farm wives in America had their favorite Cheddar recipe. There are many Cheddar variations that don't require the process called Cheddaring and are therefore quicker to make. But the flaky texture and sharp flavor of traditional Cheddar depends on this technique, in which drained curd is cut into strips, layered, and allowed to shrink as it loses whey.

Yield: 2 pounds

Ingredients:

- ❖ 2 gallons pasteurized whole milk
- ❖ ¼ teaspoon direct-set mesophilic culture or 4 tablespoons mesophilic mother culture
- ❖ ½ teaspoon liquid rennet (or ½ rennet tablet) diluted in ¼ cup cool unchlorinated water
- ❖ 4 drops annatto coloring diluted in ¼ cup unchlorinated water (optional)
- ❖ 2 tablespoons Kosher salt
- ❖ Cheese wax or vegetable shortening

1. Use a double boiler or water bath to warm the milk to 86 degrees Fahrenheit.

2. Add the culture and let it dissolve on the milk's surface for 2 minutes. Stir well using an up-and-down motion. Cover and let ripen for 40 minutes.

3. Add the diluted rennet and stir gently from top to bottom for 1 minute. Cover and let set at 86 degrees Fahrenheit for 30 minutes or until the curd gives a clean break.

4. Cut the curd into ¼-inch cubes vertically and horizontally. Use a wire whisk and skimmer to ensure that all of the curd is cut. Let set for 5 minutes.

5. Gradually raise the temperature to 100 degrees Fahrenheit over 40 minutes. Stir gently but often to keep the curd from sticking together.

6. Let the curd rest for 30 minutes at 100 degrees Fahrenheit. Stir occasionally, and let it settle to the bottom of the pot before draining.

7. Pour the curd into a muslin-lined colander with a bowl underneath, and save the whey for other recipes. Cover the colander and put it back in the warm pot for 15 minutes.

8. Place the block of curd on a cutting board, and cut it into 3-inch-wide slabs.

9. Put your pot back into a sink full of water heated to 110 degrees Fahrenheit, and layer the slabs in a crisscross pattern inside the pot.

10. Cover the pot and maintain 100 degrees Fahrenheit. Turn the slabs over and rotate them top to bottom every 15 minutes for 2 hours. Drain off the whey when you turn them.

11. After 2 hours, the slabs of curd should be small and tough. Tear them into ½-inch pieces, mix in the salt, and let them sit for about 10 minutes.

12. Pour the curd into a 2-pound muslin-lined mold. Press at medium pressure (5 to 10 pounds) for 15 minutes.

13. Take the cheese from the mold and peel off the cloth. Turn the cheese over, rewrap it, and press it at firm pressure (20 to 45 pounds) for 12 hours.

14. Repeat the turning and rewrapping. Press at firm pressure for 24 hours.

15. Remove the cheese from the mold and the cloth from the cheese. Air-dry the cheese at room temperature for 2 to 3 days or until it's dry to the touch. Turn the cheese several times a day to allow even drying.

16. Bandage or wax the Cheddar (see pages 46 and 47). Age the cheese at 50 to 55 degrees Fahrenheit and 80 to 85 percent humidity, turning it weekly. For medium Cheddar, age it for at least 6 months; for sharp Cheddar, 1 year; for extra sharp Cheddar, 18 months.

Variation: Goat's Milk Cheddar

A shorter version of the traditional recipe, this cheese has a tangier taste than cow's milk Cheddar.

Yield: 2 pounds

Ingredients:

- ❖ 2 gallons pasteurized whole goat's milk
- ❖ ¼ teaspoon direct-set mesophilic culture or 4 tablespoons mesophilic mother culture
- ❖ ½ teaspoon liquid rennet (or ½ rennet tablet) diluted in ½ cup cool unchlorinated water
- ❖ 2 tablespoons Kosher salt
- ❖ Wax or vegetable shortening

1. Use a double boiler or water bath to warm the milk to 86 degrees Fahrenheit.

2. Add the culture, let it dissolve for 2 minutes, and stir well, top to bottom. Cover and let ripen for 40 minutes.

3. Add the diluted rennet and stir gently from top to bottom for 1 minute. Cover and let set at 86 degrees Fahrenheit for 30 minutes or until you get a clean break.

4. Cut the curd into ½-inch cubes, vertically and horizontally. Let it settle for 10 minutes.

5. Gradually raise the temperature to 98 degrees Fahrenheit over about 30 minutes. Stir gently but often to keep the curd from sticking together.

6. Continue to cook the curd at 98 degrees Fahrenheit for 40 minutes, stirring gently. It should begin to mat (stick together). If it doesn't mat, keep cooking.

7. Drain off the whey, add 2 tablespoons Kosher salt to the curd, and mix well.

8. Line a 2-pound mold with muslin. Place the curds in the mold. Press at medium pressure (10 to 20 pounds) for 15 minutes.

9. Remove the cheese from the mold and peel away the cloth. Flip the cheese, rewrap it, and press at medium pressure for 1 hour.

10. Turn the cheese over and wrap it again. Press it at firm pressure (20 to 45 pounds) for 12 hours.

11. Remove the cheese from the mold and the cloth from the cheese. Air-dry the cheese at room temperature for 1 to 2 days, turning it every 6 hours. When the Cheddar is dry to the touch, you can wax or bandage it.

12. Age the cheese at 50 to 55 degrees Fahrenheit and 80 to 85 percent humidity. Turn it weekly for even ripening. Medium Cheddar should be aged at least 6 months; sharp Cheddar, 1 year; and extra sharp Cheddar, 18 months.

Variation: Sage Derby

This member of the Cheddar family, originally made in Derbyshire, England, is enhanced with aromatic green sage.

Yield: 2 pounds

Ingredients:

- ❖ 3 tablespoons chopped fresh or dried sage
- ❖ ½ cup water
- ❖ 2 gallons pasteurized whole milk
- ❖ ¼ teaspoon direct-set mesophilic culture or 4 tablespoons mesophilic mother culture
- ❖ ½ teaspoon liquid rennet (or ½ rennet tablet) diluted in ¼ cup cool unchlorinated water
- ❖ 2 tablespoons Kosher salt
- ❖ Green wax

1. Boil the sage in the water for 15 minutes, adding water to cover the herbs as needed.

2. Strain the sage and reserve the water.

3. Using a double boiler or water bath, warm the milk and sage water to 85 degrees Fahrenheit.

4. Add the culture, let it dissolve on the milk's surface for 2 minutes, and stir well. Cover and let ripen for 40 minutes at 85 degrees Fahrenheit.

5. Add the diluted rennet and stir gently from top to bottom for 1 minute. Cover and let set at 85 degrees Fahrenheit for 1 hour or until the curd is firm and separates cleanly.

6. Cut the curd into ½-inch cubes, vertically and horizontally, and let it rest for 5 minutes.

7. Gradually raise the temperature to 95 degrees Fahrenheit over about 30 minutes. Do not heat it too quickly. Stir gently but often to keep the curd from sticking together.

8. Continue to cook and stir the curd at 95 degrees Fahrenheit for 10 minutes.

9. Drain off the whey, then place the curd on a draining board, and cut it into 2-inch slices.

10. Cover the slices with a clean towel to keep them warm. Let them drain for 1 hour, turning them over every 15 minutes.

11. Tear the curd slices into 1-inch pieces. Mix in the boiled sage, and let it sit for 5 minutes. Blend in the Kosher salt.

12. Line a 2-pound mold with muslin. Place the curds in the mold and press it at medium pressure (10 to 20 pounds) for 15 minutes.

13. Remove the cheese from the mold and peel away the cloth. Flip the cheese, rewrap it, and press it at firm pressure (20 to 45 pounds) for 2 hours.

14. Turn it over again, rewrap it, and press it at firm pressure for 24 hours.

15. Remove the cheese from the mold and the cloth from the cheese. Air-dry the cheese at room temperature for 2 to 5 days or until the cheese is dry to the touch. Turn it several times a day to allow even drying.

16. Coat the cheese with green wax to match the sage.

17. Age the Cheddar at 50 to 55 degrees Fahrenheit and 80 to 85 percent humidity for at least 3 months, turning weekly.

Apple Pie with Cheddar Crust

This recipe reminds me of the old saying, "An apple pie without some cheese is like a kiss without a squeeze."

Yield: 6 to 8 servings

Ingredients:

Cheddar Crust

- ❖ 12 tablespoons (1½ sticks) unsalted butter
- ❖ 4 ounces (1 cup) sharp Cheddar, shredded
- ❖ 2 cups unbleached all-purpose flour
- ❖ ⅛ teaspoon salt
- ❖ 3 to 5 tablespoons ice water

Filling

- ❖ 6 Granny Smith apples, peeled, cored, and sliced
- ❖ ½ cup sugar
- ❖ 2 tablespoons cornstarch
- ❖ 1 teaspoon ground cinnamon
- ❖ ½ teaspoon ground nutmeg
- ❖ Juice of 1 lemon

TO MAKE THE CHEDDAR CRUST:

1. Cream the butter and Cheddar in a medium bowl using a wooden spoon.

2. Combine the flour and salt in another bowl and stir.

3. Cut the butter mixture into the flour using two knives, a pastry blender, or your hands.

4. Sprinkle 3 tablespoons of water onto the dough and stir, adding more water if needed to moisten the flour; do not overmix.

5. Turn the dough out onto a lightly floured work surface and form it into a ball.

6. Remove ⅓ of the dough, form it into a ball, flatten it into a patty about ½-inch thick, and wrap it with

plastic wrap. Flatten the remaining dough into a ½-inch-thick patty and wrap it. Refrigerate these for at least 30 minutes.

7. Preheat the oven to 375 degrees Fahrenheit. Lightly grease a 9- or 10-inch pie pan and set it aside.

8. Take the larger patty of dough from the refrigerator and place it on a lightly floured surface. Roll out the dough into a 12- to 13-inch circle.

9. Roll the dough up over the rolling pin and transfer it to the pie pan. Press the dough into the pan and cut off the excess. Refrigerate for 15 minutes.

TO MAKE THE FILLING:

1. Remove the pie pan from the refrigerator, and layer about half of the apples in concentric circles in the pie shell.

2. Mix the sugar, cornstarch, cinnamon, and nutmeg together in a small bowl. Sprinkle half of the sugar mixture over the apples.

3. Layer the remaining apples in the pan and top with the remaining sugar mixture. Sprinkle with lemon juice.

4. Remove the smaller dough patty from the refrigerator, and roll it out on a floured surface to a round slightly larger than the top of the pie. Cut the dough into strips about 1-inch wide using a knife or a pastry cutter.

5. Weave the strips to form a lattice pattern on top of the pie. Trim the ends of the strips if necessary. Crimp the edges of the bottom crust and the lattice together by pinching the dough.

6. Put the pie pan on a baking sheet, place it in the oven, and bake for 40 to 50 minutes, or until the apples are bubbling and the crust is golden brown. Remove from the oven and let cool.

Twice-Baked Potatoes

Yield: 6 to 8 servings

Ingredients:

- 4 large russet potatoes
- 8 slices bacon (optional)
- 1 cup sour cream (see recipe on page 59)
- ½ cup whole milk
- 4 tablespoons butter
- ½ teaspoon salt
- ½ teaspoon pepper
- 1 cup shredded Cheddar cheese
- 8 green onions, sliced

1. Preheat oven to 350 degrees Fahrenheit.

2. Bake the potatoes in the preheated oven for 1 hour.

3. Place the bacon in a large, deep skillet and cook over medium-high heat until it's evenly brown. Drain, crumble, and set aside.

4. When the potatoes are done, allow them to cool for 10 minutes. Slice them in half lengthwise and scoop the flesh into a large bowl; save the skins.

5. To the potato flesh, add the sour cream, milk, butter, salt, pepper, ½ cup of the cheese, and half of the green onions. Mix everything together using a hand mixer until it's well blended and creamy.

6. Spoon the mixture into the potato skins and top each with the remaining cheese, green onions, and bacon.

7. Bake for another 15 minutes.

Cantal

Native to the Auvergne, where it was originally shaped in beechwood molds, Cantal is one of the world's oldest cheeses. Romans feasted on it when they conquered Gaul. The elder Pliny noted this savory event in his Naturalis Historia, written nearly 2,000 years ago. Cantal can be eaten young and sweet or well aged and dry. Though this is a 2-pound recipe, French Cantal weighs a hefty 88 pounds, Petit Cantal weighs 44 pounds, and baby brother Cantalet weighs 22 pounds.

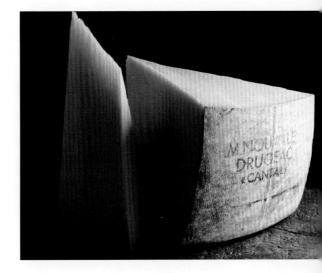

Yield: 2 pounds

Ingredients:

❖ 2 gallons pasteurized whole milk

❖ ¼ teaspoon direct-set mesophilic culture or 4 tablespoons mesophilic mother culture

❖ ½ teaspoon liquid rennet (or ¼ rennet tablet) diluted in ¼ cup cool unchlorinated water

❖ 2 tablespoons Kosher salt

1. In a double boiler or water bath, warm the milk to 86 degrees Fahrenheit.

2. Add the culture, let it dissolve on the milk for 2 minutes, and stir well from top to bottom. Cover and let ripen for 15 minutes at 86 degrees Fahrenheit.

3. Add the diluted rennet and stir gently from top to bottom for 1 minute. Cover and let set at 86 degrees Fahrenheit for 1 hour or until the curd gives a clean break.

4. Cut the curd into ¼-inch cubes, using a whisk to catch any pieces you miss and a skimmer to lift the curd. Let settle for 5 minutes.

5. Line a colander with muslin (place a catch bowl underneath), and pour the curd and whey into it. Catch the whey in a large bowl if you are making ricotta. Keep the curd warm while it drains—about 20 minutes.

6. Line a 2-pound mold with muslin, and break the curd into several pieces as you pile it in. Press at light pressure (5 to 10 pounds) for 12 hours.

7. Remove the cheese from the press and the cloth from the cheese. Turn the cheese over and rewrap it. Continue to press at light pressure for another 12 hours.

8. In a large bowl, mill (break up) the cheese into 1-inch pieces, add the salt and mix well, kneading with your fingers.

9. Rinse your muslin and mold, replace the salted cheese in the mold, and press at firm pressure (20 to 45 pounds) for 2 to 3 days. Every 24 hours, turn the cheese over, rewrap it, and continue pressing at firm pressure.

10. Remove the cheese from the mold and the cloth from the cheese. Air-dry the cheese at room temperature for 2 to 3 days, flipping it every 6 hours.

11. When the cheese is dry to your touch, age it at 50 to 55 degrees Fahrenheit and 80 to 85 percent humidity for 3 to 6 months. Twice a week, turn the cheese and wipe the rind with a brine solution (1 cup boiled water and 2 teaspoons Kosher salt, chilled).

Cauliflower-Cheese Soup

This soup is the perfect comfort food for a winter afternoon. You can substitute any semi-hard whole-milk cheese for Cantal.

Yield: 6 servings

Ingredients:

- 1 medium potato, peeled and diced (makes about 2 cups)
- 1 medium cauliflower, cut into florets (separate and set aside 2 cups of florets)
- 1 medium carrot, peeled and chopped
- 3 garlic cloves, peeled
- 1½ cups onion, chopped
- 1½ teaspoons salt

- ✤ 4 cups water
- ✤ 2 cups grated Cantal
- ✤ ¾ cup whole or low-fat milk
- ✤ 1 teaspoon dill
- ✤ ½ teaspoon caraway seeds
- ✤ Black pepper to taste
- ✤ ½ cup grated Cantal (to garnish)

1. Add the potato, cauliflower, carrot, garlic, onion, salt, and water to a large saucepan.

2. Bring the water to a boil, and simmer until the vegetables are very tender. Purée the mixture in a food processor, and then transfer it to a soup pot.

3. Steam the 2 cups of cauliflower you set aside until they are tender. Add these and the remaining ingredients to your soup.

4. Heat the soup gently and serve with a cheese garnish.

Monterey Jack

What we call Monterey Jack, or just Jack, cheese was brought to the Americas by Franciscan monks in the eighteenth century. A cheese maker in Monterey named Domingo Pedrazzi used a cheese press called a house jack to make it, and the name stuck. Most Jack is semi-hard, but if you want a hard grating cheese, substitute skim milk for whole milk and age it at least a year, whereby it becomes Dry Jack.

Yield: 1 to 2 pounds

Ingredients:

- ✤ 2 gallons pasteurized whole milk
- ✤ ¼ teaspoon direct-set mesophilic culture or 4 tablespoons mesophilic mother culture
- ✤ ½ teaspoon liquid rennet (or ½ rennet tablet) diluted in ¼ cup unchlorinated water
- ✤ 1 tablespoon Kosher salt
- ✤ Wax or vegetable oil

1. Use a double boiler or water bath to warm the milk to 90 degrees Fahrenheit.

2. Add the culture, let it dissolve on the milk's surface, and stir well, top to bottom. Cover and let ripen at 90 degrees Fahrenheit for 45 minutes.

3. Add the diluted rennet and stir gently from top to bottom for 1 minute.

4. Cover and let the milk set at 90 degrees Fahrenheit for 40 minutes or until the curd gives a clean break.

5. Cut the curd into ¼-inch cubes, using a whisk to catch any pieces you miss and a skimmer to lift the curd. Let set for another 40 minutes at 90 degrees Fahrenheit.

6. Gradually raise the temperature to 100 degrees Fahrenheit over about 30 minutes. Stir gently but often to keep the curd from sticking together.

7. Hold the curd at 100 degrees Fahrenheit for 30 minutes, stirring occasionally. Let it rest for 5 minutes.

8. Pour off the whey to the level of the curd, and allow the curd to set 30 minutes longer, stirring every 5 minutes to prevent sticking. Maintain at 100 degrees Fahrenheit.

9. Line a colander with damp muslin, and place it in a catch bowl. Spoon the curd into the colander.

10. Sprinkle the Kosher salt over the curd, mixing gently. Let drain.

11. Line a 2-pound mold with muslin and fill it with curd. Press the cheese with a 4-pound weight for 15 minutes. (A filled half-gallon plastic water jug weighs 4 pounds.)

12. Remove the cheese from the mold and carefully peel away the cloth. Turn the cheese over, rewrap it, and press it at medium pressure (10 to 20 pounds) for 12 hours.

13. Remove the cheese and place it on a clean cheese board to air-dry at room temperature. Turn it twice a day until its surface is dry to the touch. Drying may take up to 3 days, depending on temperature and humidity.

14. Wax or oil the cheese and allow it to age at 50 to 55 degrees Fahrenheit and 80 to 85 percent humidity for 1 to 4 months, turning it weekly. The longer it ages, the sharper the taste.

Variation: Pepper Jack

This is a spicy twist on Monterey Jack. You'll need the following ingredients in addition to those listed in the original recipe. Follow the Monterey Jack recipe, but add in the ingredients and steps below.

Ingredients:

❖ 1 teaspoon hot chili flakes

❖ ½ cup water

1. Before heating the milk, boil pepper flakes in water for 10 minutes.

2. Strain and remove the chili flakes.

3. Add the pepper water to your milk and follow the remaining steps.

4. When you get to step 10, stir in the boiled pepper flakes with the Kosher salt.

Quesadillas Deluxe

Queso is Spanish for "cheese," and these cheese tortillas are a popular Mexican snack food. Create your own version of this dish by adding some of the suggested ingredients. This recipe feeds two people, so increase portions as needed.

Yield: 2 servings

Ingredients:

❖ Olive oil or grapeseed oil

❖ 2 large flour tortillas

❖ 1 cup grated Monterey Jack

Optional Ingredients:

❖ ½ cup mushrooms, sliced

❖ 1 green onion, chopped

❖ Black olives, sliced

❖ Fresh tomatoes, diced

❖ 8 to 12 ounces of chicken, beef, pork, or fish, roughly chopped

1. Heat a cast iron frying pan to medium-high heat. Add a small amount of oil.

2. Place one of the tortillas in the pan and flip it several times with a spatula until air pockets begin to form in the tortilla.

3. Take ½ cup of the grated Monterey Jack and sprinkle it over the top of the tortilla, making sure the cheese doesn't land on the pan. Add your selected optional ingredients, spreading them evenly over the cheese.

4. Reduce the heat to low and cover the pan for a minute or two. You want the cheese to melt, but you don't want to burn the tortilla.

5. When the cheese has melted, use a spatula to lift up ½ of the quesadilla and flip it over, as if you were making an omelet.

6. The quesadilla is done when slightly browned. Remove it from the pan and cut it into wedges. Serve with salsa, sour cream, and guacamole.

7. Repeat the previous steps for the second quesadilla.

Cotswold

Here is a variation of the English cheese Double Gloucester, made in the Cotswolds region of England. Chives and onions bring a distinctive flavor to its firm texture.

Yield: 2 pounds

Ingredients:

❖ 2 teaspoons dried onion

❖ 2 teaspoons dried chives

❖ ½ cup water

❖ 2 gallons pasteurized whole milk

❖ ¼ teaspoon thermophilic culture or 4 tablespoons thermophilic mother culture

❖ ½ teaspoon liquid rennet (or ½ rennet tablet) diluted in ¼ cup cool unchlorinated water

❖ 4 drops annatto coloring diluted in ¼ cup unchlorinated water

1. Boil the onion and chives in the water for 15 minutes, adding water to cover as needed.

2. Strain the onion and chives and reserve the water.

3. In a double boiler or water bath, warm the milk and flavored water to 90 degrees Fahrenheit.

4. Add the culture, let it dissolve on the milk's surface for 2 minutes, and stir well. Cover and let ripen for 45 minutes at 90 degrees Fahrenheit.

5. Add the diluted annatto coloring and stir, top to bottom.

6. Add the diluted rennet and stir gently from top to bottom for 1 minute. Cover and let set at 90 degrees Fahrenheit for 45 minutes or until you get a clean break.

7. Cut the curd into ¼-inch cubes, using a whisk to catch any pieces you miss and a skimmer to lift the curd. Stir for 20 minutes at 90 degrees Fahrenheit.

8. Gradually raise the temperature to 104 degrees Fahrenheit over about 40 minutes. Stir gently but often to keep the curd from sticking together.

9. Hold the curd at 104 degrees Fahrenheit for 30 minutes, stirring occasionally. Let it rest for 5 minutes.

10. Line a colander with muslin, pour the curd into the colander, and let the whey drain into a catch bowl until it stops.

11. Pour the curd into a 2-pound cloth-lined mold. Press at light pressure (5 to 10 pounds) for 15 minutes.

12. Remove the cheese from the mold and peel away the cloth. Flip the cheese, rewrap it, and press at medium pressure (10 to 20 pounds) for 15 minutes.

13. Again, unwrap the cheese, turn it, and rewrap it. Press at firm pressure (20 to 45 pounds) for 24 hours.

14. Remove the cheese from the mold and the cloth from the cheese. Air-dry the cheese at room temperature for 2 to 5 days or until the cheese is dry to your touch.

15. Wax the cheese or allow it to form a natural rind. For a natural rind, brush or wipe the cheese with a brine solution to remove any mold.

16. Age the cheese at 55 degrees Fahrenheit and 80 to 85 percent humidity for 1 to 3 months, turning it weekly.

Caerphilly

From South Wales comes this fresh cheese (pronounced CAR-filly) that matures in only 3 weeks. For that reason, Caerphilly was a Welsh miner's favorite lunch. It has a tender, almost crumbly, white paste (the inside of the cheese). For this recipe, you will let the pressed cheese soak in a brine bath.

Yield: 2 pounds

Ingredients:

❖ 1 gallon water

❖ 2 pounds Kosher salt

❖ 2 gallons pasteurized whole milk

❖ ¼ teaspoon direct-set mesophilic culture or 4 tablespoons mesophilic mother culture

❖ ½ teaspoon liquid rennet (or ½ rennet tablet) diluted in ¼ cup cool unchlorinated water

❖ Brine bath (see page 76)

1. In a double boiler or water bath, warm the milk to 88 degrees Fahrenheit.

2. Add the culture, let it dissolve on the milk's surface for 2 minutes, and stir well. Cover and let ripen for 45 minutes at 88 degrees Fahrenheit.

3. Add the diluted rennet and stir gently from top to bottom for 1 minute. Cover and let set at 88 degrees Fahrenheit for 45 minutes or until the curd gives a clean break.

4. Cut the curd into ¼-inch cubes, using a whisk to catch any pieces you miss and a skimmer to lift the curd. Let rest for 5 minutes.

5. Slowly raise the milk's temperature to 95 degrees Fahrenheit, stirring gently. This should take no less than 30 minutes.

6. Leave the curd undisturbed at 95 degrees Fahrenheit for 40 minutes.

7. Line a colander with muslin, place a catch bowl beneath it, pour in the curd, and let it drain for 5 minutes. Reserve the whey.

8. Line a 2-pound mold with muslin. Mill (break up) the curd mass into 1-inch pieces and pack the mold with it. Press at light pressure (5 to 10 pounds) for 30 minutes.

9. Remove the cheese from the press and the cloth from the cheese. Turn over the cheese, rewrap it, and press it at medium pressure (10 to 20 pounds) for 4 hours.

10. Remove the cheese from the press and the cloth from the cheese. Turn over the cheese, rewrap it, and press it at firm pressure (20 to 45 pounds) for 8 hours.

11. Remove the cheese from the press, and soak it in the brine bath for 10 hours, turning the cheese once.

12. Take the cheese from the brine bath and air-dry it at room temperature for 2 to 3 days, turning it every 6 hours.

13. When the cheese is dry to your touch, age it at 55 degrees Fahrenheit and 80 to 85 percent humidity, turning it over daily. It will be ready to eat after 3 weeks. If you want sharper flavor, let the cheese cure—waxed or with a natural rind—for up to 4 months.

Caciotta

If you can get sheep's milk, this recipe reproduces an Italian favorite with luscious, buttery consistency and the sparkle of saffron. You can combine sheep's and cow's milk, but the result won't be as flavorful. Be sure to buy high-quality saffron threads that are long and deep red—it's worth the investment. In Umbria, cheese makers mix their sheep's milk curd with black truffles and call their truffled delicacy Caciotta al Tartufo.

Yield: 3 to 4 pounds

Ingredients:

- ❖ 1 gallon water
- ❖ 2 pounds Kosher salt
- ❖ 2 gallons pasteurized sheep's milk
- ❖ Several saffron threads
- ❖ ¼ teaspoon direct-set mesophilic culture or 4 tablespoons mother culture
- ❖ ¼ teaspoon liquid rennet (or ½ rennet tablet) diluted in ¼ cup cool unchlorinated water
- ❖ Brine bath (see page 76)

1. In a double boiler or water bath, warm the milk and saffron to 90 degrees Fahrenheit. Stir gently.

2. Add the culture and let it dissolve for 5 minutes before mixing from top to bottom. Remove the saffron, if desired. Cover and let ripen for 30 minutes.

3. Keeping the milk temperature at 90 degrees Fahrenheit, add the diluted rennet and stir gently from

top to bottom for 1 minute. Cover and let set at 90 degrees Fahrenheit for 40 minutes or until the curd gives a clean break.

4. Cut the curd into ½-inch cubes, and let it rest for 5 minutes.

5. Slowly raise the milk's temperature to 95 degrees Fahrenheit over about 20 minutes. Do not heat too quickly.

6. Stir the curd at 95 degrees Fahrenheit for 20 minutes to keep it from sticking together. Let it rest for 5 minutes.

7. Line a colander with muslin, place a catch bowl underneath, and pour in the curd. Let it drain for 30 minutes.

8. Break up the curd with your fingers as you transfer it to a mold, and then move the mold to your cheese press. Press at light pressure (5 to 10 pounds) for 15 minutes.

9. Remove the cheese from the mold and the cloth from the cheese. Turn the cheese over, rewrap it, and press it at medium pressure (10 to 20 pounds) for 6 hours.

10. Transfer the cheese from the press to the brine bath and leave for 4 hours, turning it over after 2 hours.

11. Remove the cheese from the brine, pat it dry, and ripen it at 50 to 55 degrees Fahrenheit and 85 percent humidity for 4 weeks. It will continue to drain, so take care to wipe up any whey in your ripening container and to turn the cheese daily during the first week. Caciotta can be ripened with a natural rind or waxed after the first week.

Caciotta and Fagioli Salad

Italians celebrate spring and the appearance at market of young sheep's milk cheeses with this simple meal.

Yield: 4 servings

Ingredients:

- ½ pound fresh fava beans
- ½ pound Caciotta, cut into ½-inch cubes
- Extra virgin olive oil, preferably cold-pressed
- 2 small heads of radicchio, torn
- Salt and pepper

1. Shell the beans. Steam them for several minutes, allow them to cool, and remove their skins.

2. Combine the cubed cheese and the beans. Sprinkle with olive oil, salt and pepper to taste, and serve on a bed of radicchio.

CHAPTER 8

Washed Curds

The semi-hard cheeses in this chapter boast Cheddarlike flavor but are moister and milder thanks to a process called *washing the curd*. After the milk is ripened and the curd cut, whey is replaced in the cooking pot with hot water. This washes milk sugar (lactose) from the curd and lowers the acid level to avoid souring the cheese. Washing the curd allows it to cure faster. Washed-curd cheeses such as Colby and Gouda can be ready for eating in three months. Before you dive into the recipes in this chapter, you may want to review the techniques for molding, pressing, and aging cheese in chapter 3.

> "Cheese making is a life process, not just a technique."
>
> —Abe Madey, Hawthorne Valley Farm

The Dutch adopted and refined the technique of "washing" cut curd with hot water, which creates a cheese with a sweet taste and texture; small "eyes," or holes; and a close-knit, tight rind. Wisconsin cheese makers specialize in the Dutch tradition of "washed curd" cheeses such as Gouda and Edam; one of the best is Paul Reigle of Maple Leaf, a farmer-owned cooperative that's been around since 1910. "Our company," says Reigle, "is still locally farmer-owned, and some of our families are now in their second and third generation with us." Maple Leaf crafts a 12-pound wheel of Gouda, naturally smoked over hickory chips. That's real smoke, not liquid. In Monroe, Wisconsin, Emmi Roth USA boasts a line of Dutch-style cheeses—smoked and non-smoked Gouda aged at least six months and a part-skim Edam—that it calls Vintage Van Gogh.

Washed-Curd Cheese Recipes

For all washed-curd cheeses, increase the heat when recipes call for it by no more than 2 degrees every 5 minutes. Several of these recipes require you to soak the cheese in a brine bath (see page 76).

Colby

Named for a township in Southern Wisconsin, Colby is one of few cheeses "born in the USA." Its cousin, Colby Longhorn, refers to the long, cylindrical molds used to shape the cheese, not to the Longhorn cow.

Yield: 2 pounds

Ingredients:

- 2 gallons pasteurized whole milk
- ¼ teaspoon direct-set mesophilic culture or 4 tablespoons mesophilic mother culture
- ½ teaspoon liquid rennet (or ½ rennet tablet) diluted in ¼ cup cool unchlorinated water
- 4 drops annatto coloring diluted in ¼ cup unchlorinated water (optional)
- Cheese wax
- Brine bath

1. Use a double boiler or water bath to heat the milk to 86 degrees Fahrenheit.
2. Add the culture, let it dissolve on the milk's surface for 2 minutes, and then stir it well from top to bottom. Cover and let ripen for 1 hour.

3. Add the coloring and mix well (optional).

4. Keeping the milk's temperature at 86 degrees Fahrenheit, add the diluted rennet and stir gently from top to bottom for 1 minute. Cover and let set for 30 minutes or until the curd is firm and separates cleanly.

5. Cut the curd into ½-inch cubes, vertically and horizontally, in a grid pattern. Let them set for 5 minutes.

6. Gradually raise the temperature to 102 degrees Fahrenheit over about 40 minutes. Do not heat too quickly. Stir gently but often to keep the curd from sticking together.

7. Allow the curd to settle and rest for about 15 minutes.

8. Drain off the whey to the level of the curd. Replace with the same amount of water, heated to 102 degrees Fahrenheit, and stir for 2 minutes.

9. Cover the curd and let it rest for about 15 minutes.

10. Pour the curd and whey into a muslin-lined colander with a catch bowl beneath it. Keep the curd warm while you allow it to drain for 20 minutes.

11. Line a 2-pound mold with muslin. Break up the curd into ½-inch bits, and place them in the mold. Press at medium pressure (10 to 20 pounds) for 30 minutes.

12. Remove the cheese from the mold and peel away the cloth. Flip the cheese, rewrap it, and press at firm pressure (20 to 45 pounds) for 12 hours or overnight.

13. Unwrap the cheese and place it in a brine bath for 12 hours, turning it over after 6 hours.

14. Let the cheese dry on a mat or board at room temperature for 2 to 3 days or until dry to the touch, turning it over several times a day.

15. Coat the cheese with two or three layers of wax, and age it for 2 to 3 months at 50 to 55 degrees Fahrenheit and 85 percent humidity. Turn it weekly to distribute the fat and moisture evenly.

Gouda

Gouda is named for a little town near Rotterdam, but it has been a big winner for Holland. It accounts for more than 60 percent of that country's cheese production. Exports are coated in red wax and wrapped in cellophane. In Europe,

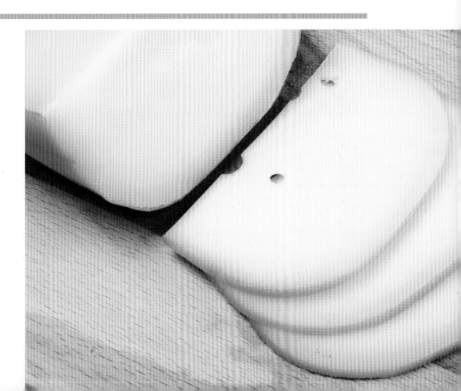

mature Gouda (aged more than 18 months) is coated in black wax. But Gouda is also sold with herbs (green wax), peppercorns (brown wax), and caraway (pale orange wax). Like all washed-curd cheeses, Gouda can be eaten after 3 months, but longer aging intensifies its flavor.

Yield: 2 pounds

Ingredients:

❖ 2 gallons pasteurized whole milk

❖ ¼ teaspoon direct-set mesophilic culture or 4 tablespoons mesophilic mother culture

❖ ½ teaspoon liquid rennet (or ½ rennet tablet) diluted in ¼ cup unchlorinated water

❖ Brine bath

❖ Cheese wax

1. Use a double boiler or water bath to warm the milk to 86 degrees Fahrenheit.

2. Add the culture, let it dissolve on the milk's surface for 2 minutes, and stir well from top to bottom. Cover and let ripen for 10 minutes.

3. Keeping the milk's temperature at 86 degrees Fahrenheit, add the diluted rennet and stir gently from top to bottom for 1 minute. Cover and let set for 1 hour or until the curd is firm and separates cleanly.

4. Cut the curd into ½-inch cubes. Let the cubes set for 15 minutes, stirring occasionally. Curd should sink to the bottom of the pot.

5. Drain off a third of the whey. Stir the curd while you add water, heated to 140 degrees Fahrenheit, until the temperature reaches 92 degrees Fahrenheit.

6. Let the curd rest for 15 minutes, stirring occasionally.

7. Drain off the whey to the level of the curd. Stir the curd while you add water (again, heated to 140 degrees Fahrenheit) until the temperature in the pot reaches 100 degrees Fahrenheit.

8. Stir for 15 minutes at 100 degrees Fahrenheit, and then let rest for 10 minutes.

9. Pour the curds and whey into a muslin-lined colander with a catch bowl underneath. Keep the curds warm while you allow them to drain for 20 minutes.

10. Line a 2-pound mold with muslin. Break the curd into ½-inch bits, and place them in the mold. Press at medium pressure (10 to 20 pounds) for 30 minutes.

11. Remove the cheese from the mold and peel away the cloth. Flip the cheese, rewrap it, and press at firm pressure (20 to 45 pounds) for 12 hours or overnight.

12. Unwrap the cheese and place it in a brine bath for 12 hours, turning it after 6 hours.

13. Let the cheese dry on a mat or board at room temperature for 2 to 3 days or until dry to the touch, turning it over several times a day.

14. Place the cheese on a clean mat in a ripening container to cure at 50 to 55 degrees Fahrenheit and 85 percent humidity. For a natural rind, wipe the rind with brine (1 cup boiled water and 2 teaspoons Kosher salt, mixed and chilled) every 2 days to inhibit mold. You can age Gouda indefinitely, or you can coat the cheese with wax and age it for up to 6 months. Turn the cheese weekly while it ages to distribute the fat and moisture evenly.

Variation: Gouda with Mustard or Caraway Seeds

To the original ingredients, add:

❖ 1 tablespoon mustard seed or caraway seed

❖ ½ cup water

1. Boil the seeds in the water for 15 minutes, adding water to keep them covered if necessary.

2. Strain the seeds and reserve the water. Allow the water to cool.

3. Add the flavored water to the milk at the beginning of the original recipe, and follow steps 1 through 9.

4. When the curd has drained, add the seeds and blend well.

5. Follow steps 10 through 14.

Corn and Gouda Custard

Fresh corn kernels, cream, and cheese make a savory custard. Note that 4 ounces of solid Gouda is equal to 1 cup of grated Gouda.

Yield: 6 servings

Ingredients:

- ❖ Butter
- ❖ 1¼ cup heavy cream
- ❖ 1 cup whole milk
- ❖ 1¾ cups grated (7 ounces ungrated) Gouda
- ❖ 1 cup fresh breadcrumbs
- ❖ 3 egg yolks
- ❖ 1 cup fresh corn kernels
- ❖ 1 teaspoon salt
- ❖ ½ teaspoon fresh ground pepper
- ❖ 2 pinches crushed red pepper flakes

1. Preheat oven to 400 degrees Fahrenheit, and butter a 10-by-7-inch baking dish; set aside.
2. Heat the cream and milk over medium heat until simmering.
3. Reduce the heat to low, and stir in 1½ cups of the cheese until it's melted.
4. Add the breadcrumbs and remove the mixture from heat. Let cool.
5. Whisk in the egg yolks, ¾ cup of the corn, and then the salt, black pepper, and crushed red pepper flakes.
6. Pour the custard into your baking dish and top it with the remaining ¼ cup of corn and ¼ cup of cheese.
7. Place the dish in a large roasting pan. Add 1 inch of hot water to the pan, and bake until the custard sets, about 1 hour.

Edam

With its trademark red wax and circular shape, Edam is unmistakable on any cheese tray. It's named for the town of Edam in North Holland province, and its consistency is drier than Gouda because it's made with low-fat milk. This cheese is surrounded with colorful history. Rounds of Edam were used as cannon balls by Uruguay to defeat Brazil in a nineteenth-century naval battle, it was eaten to ward off plague in the Middle Ages, and it was recovered from Robert Falcon Scott's ill-fated expedition to the South Pole 44 years later, still edible.

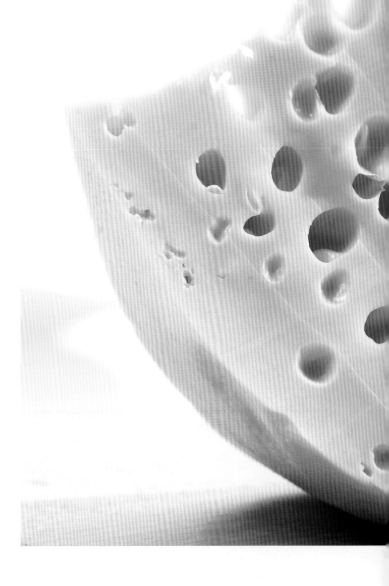

Yield: 1½ pounds

Ingredients:

❖ 2 gallons pasteurized low-fat milk

❖ ¼ teaspoon direct-set mesophilic culture or 4 tablespoons mesophilic mother culture

❖ ½ teaspoon liquid rennet (or ½ rennet tablet) diluted in ¼ cup unchlorinated water

❖ Brine bath

❖ Cheese wax

1. Use a double boiler or water bath to warm the milk to 88 degrees Fahrenheit.

2. Add the culture, let it dissolve for 2 minutes on the milk's surface. Stir well from top to bottom. Cover and let ripen for 10 minutes.

3. Keeping the milk's temperature at 88 degrees Fahrenheit, add the diluted rennet and stir gently from top to bottom for 1 minute. Cover and let set for 45 minutes or until the curd is firm and separates cleanly.

4. Cut the curd into ½-inch cubes, vertically and horizontally, in a grid pattern. Let the cubes rest for 5 minutes.

5. Gradually warm the temperature of the curd to 92 degrees Fahrenheit over about 20 minutes. Stir gently and do not heat too quickly. Let the curd settle for 5 minutes.

6. Drain off the whey to the level of the curd. Replace with an equal amount of water, heated to 110 degrees Fahrenheit, until the temperature in the pot reaches 98 degrees Fahrenheit.

7. Continue to stir the curd at 98 degrees Fahrenheit for 30 minutes, and then let it rest for 5 minutes.

8. Drain off the additional whey into a cooking pot and heat it to 125 degrees Fahrenheit. Keep the whey at that temperature.

9. Line a 2-pound mold with muslin, gently place the curds in the mold, and press at medium pressure (10 to 20 pounds) for 30 minutes.

10. Remove the cheese from the mold and peel away the cloth. Set the cheese in the whey bath for 20 minutes, turning it a few times.

11. Remove the cheese from the whey bath, rewrap it in muslin, and put it back in the mold. Press at firm pressure (20 to 45 pounds) for 6 hours.

12. Flip the cheese, rewrap it, and press it at firm pressure for another 6 hours.

13. Soak the cheese in the brine bath for 12 hours, turning it once.

14. Remove the cheese from the brine and pat it dry. Let the cheese dry on a mat or board at room temperature for 2 to 3 days or until it's dry to the touch, turning it over several times a day.

15. Wax the cheese or age it with a natural rind at 50 to 55 degrees Fahrenheit and 85 percent humidity for 2 months. Turn it weekly to ensure even ripening. For a natural rind, wipe the cheese with brine (1 cup boiled water and 2 teaspoons Kosher salt, mixed and chilled) every 2 days to inhibit mold.

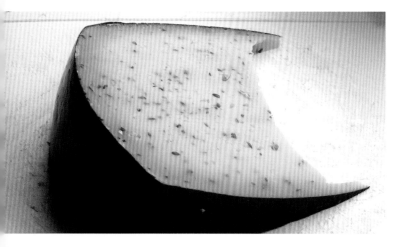

Variation: Leiden

A variation on Edam, this low-fat cheese uses cumin and caraway as flavoring and is named for the Dutch city of Leiden.

To the ingredients for Edam, add:

❖ 1 teaspoon cumin seed

❖ 1 teaspoon caraway seed

❖ ½ cup water

1. Boil the seeds in water for 15 minutes, adding water to keep them covered if necessary.

2. Strain the seeds and reserve the water. Allow the water to cool.

3. Add the water to the milk at the beginning of the original recipe, and follow steps 1 through 8.

4. When the curd has drained, add the seeds and blend well.

5. Follow steps 9 through 15.

Edam Veggie Burgers

Never has a protein-rich meatless meal tasted so good. Tomato chutney adds a yummy finishing touch.

Yield: 4 servings

Ingredients:

❖ 3 ounces pine nuts

❖ 1 can (425 grams) cannellini beans, drained and rinsed

❖ 4 ounces Edam cheese, cut into very small cubes

❖ ½ cup onion, minced

❖ ½ tablespoon sun-dried tomato paste

❖ 1 egg, beaten

❖ 2½ ounces fresh breadcrumbs

❖ Several tablespoons of olive or grapeseed oil

1. Lightly toast the pine nuts over medium heat for 2 to 3 minutes or until golden. Remove from pan and set aside.

2. Place the beans in a large bowl and mash well. Add the Edam bits, pine nuts, onion, tomato paste, egg, and a third of the breadcrumbs. Season to taste, and gently mix everything together until the ingredients are thoroughly combined.

3. Shape the mixture into 8 burgers. Coat the outside of each burger with the remaining breadcrumbs. Cover and chill the patties in the fridge for 20 minutes.

4. Heat the oil in a large frying pan and add the burgers. Fry each burger for 3 to 4 minutes on each side until golden and heated through. Drain the finished burgers on brown paper.

5. Serve on a bed of mixed greens with tomato chutney.

CHAPTER 9

Washed Rinds

When the Great Fire of London broke out in 1666, Samuel Pepys, a devotee of stinky cheeses, took care to bury his prized "Parmazan" cheese in the garden, never mind the wife and house. Lovers of stinky cheese are legion, but not everyone wants one for a seatmate. Maybe that's why Époisses and its divinely repulsive odor have been banned from public transportation in France. Too smelly even for the French? Now that's bad.

Another candidate for the Smelly Cheese Award is Stinking Bishop—not named for a clergyman, as you might suspect, but for an offensive member of Gloucestershire's Bishop family. The Bishops make a local perry (fermented pear juice) used to wash the curd and rind of Stinking Bishop rounds. The result? Far from fruity, its powerful aroma has been known to raise the dead.

What gives cheeses such as Taleggio, Livarot, Pont-l'Évêque, Vacherin, and Limburger their notorious odor also enhances their flavor: it's the addition of ripening bacteria called *Brevibacterium linens*. Often, a pinch of *Geotrichum candidum* is added with *B. linens,* as well.

> **"The rankest compound of villainous smell That ever offended a nostril."**
> —*Shakespeare on Limburger*

In my recipes, you'll add the bacteria directly to the milk, but other recipes often call for the cheese maker to spray it onto the cheese using an atomizer. Afterwards, the rind is washed regularly with a brine-soaked cloth to encourage the growth of microflora. Surface microflora composed of bacteria and yeast produce a reddish orange *smear*, and cheeses crafted this way are often called *smear-ripened*.

For award-winning examples of American washed-rind cheese, try a few from Cato Corner Farm of Colchester, Connecticut, including Hooligan, Drunken Hooligan (rubbed in wine grapes), Drunk Monk (bathed in brown ale), and Despearado (soused in pear mash and *eau-de-vie*).

After soaking the cheese in one brine, you'll wash it in another brine solution.

RIND WASHING

In addition to soaking the cheeses in a brine bath (see page 76), you'll also have to wash the rinds with a brine solution. Here's how.

1. Always use a fresh brine solution of 1 cup boiled water and 2 teaspoons Kosher salt. Cool before applying it to the cheese.

2. Dip a clean cloth or sponge into the brine and squeeze it out.

3. Rub the cheese all over with the damp cloth; don't soak it.

4. Discard the used brine (unlike soaking brine, you cannot reuse washing brine).

DRAINING THE CURD

A few of the cheeses in this chapter aren't pressed. Instead, the curd is placed in molds between two mats in a draining pan, flipped in its mold, and allowed to drain for up to 24 hours. Perform this trick carefully so as not to tear the curd.

Cheese in molds draining on a rack.

1. Slide one hand underneath the bottom mat, and place the other on the top mat.

2. Hold the mold tightly between the two mats, lift everything at once, and flip it all over quickly.

3. Set the mold back in the draining pan.

4. Lift up the top mat to ensure it isn't stuck to the curd.

PROPER AGING

High humidity (90 percent) and a temperature no colder than 55 degrees Fahrenheit are essential for smear-ripened cheese. Anything less and the *B. linens* bacteria won't grow. As the cheese ripens, you will wash it in brine (or beer, wine, or brandy) to encourage a firm and pungent rind. Though the exteriors of these cheeses are pungent, the paste (interior) is soft and even creamy. The best news? Washed-rind cheeses are ready to eat after only 1 to 2 months.

Washed-Rind Cheese Recipes

For all washed-rind cheeses, increase the heat when recipes call for it by no more than 2 degrees every 5 minutes. Several of these recipes require that you soak the cheese in a brine bath (see page 76 for instructions), and all require washing in brine (see page 118).

Muenster

From the Latin word for monastery, Muenster owes its origins—like so many cheeses—to the skill and inventiveness of monks. In this case, the skill of Benedictine monks, who stirred their cow's milk curd within sight of the Vosges Mountains of Alsace-Lorraine in northeastern France. In France, Muenster is protected by certification and is typically served with new potatoes, boiled in their skins. How did American Muenster become so bland? I don't know, but *vive la différence*!

Muenster is not pressed. Instead, it's turned over in its mold and allowed to drain until firm. Perform this trick by holding the mold between two draining mats. Lift it, flip it over, and set it back in the draining pan.

Yield: 2 pounds

Ingredients:

❖ 2 gallons pasteurized whole milk

❖ ¼ teaspoon direct-set mesophilic culture or 4 tablespoons mesophilic mother culture

❖ ⅛ teaspoon *Brevibacterium linens*

❖ Tiny pinch *Geotrichum candidum*

❖ ½ teaspoon liquid rennet (or ½ rennet tablet) diluted in ¼ cup unchlorinated water

❖ 1 teaspoon Kosher salt

❖ Brine solution for rind washing

1. Use a double boiler or water bath to warm the milk to 90 degrees Fahrenheit.

2. Add the culture, *B. linens*, and *G. candidum.* Let them dissolve on the milk's surface for 5 minutes. Stir gently from top to bottom.

3. Keeping the milk's temperature at 90 degrees Fahrenheit, add the diluted rennet and stir gently for 1 minute. Cover and let set for 40 minutes or until the curd is firm and separates cleanly.

4. Cut the curd into ½-inch cubes. Let it settle for 5 minutes.

5. Gradually raise the temperature of the curd to 100 degrees Fahrenheit, taking no less than 30 minutes. Stir to prevent matting. Keep the curd at 100 degrees for another 30 minutes, then let settle.

6. Carefully pour the curd into a muslin-lined colander with a catch bowl beneath. Allow it to drain for 20 minutes.

7. Line a 2-pound mold (or two 1-pound molds) with muslin. Ladle the curd into the mold, set the mold on a mat in a draining pan, and cover. Let the curds drain at room temperature for 24 hours. Flip the cheese in its mold several times during this period by holding the mold between two mats and turning it over. Keep the cheese well covered and in a warm place.

8. If the cheese is still soft after 24 hours, keep draining. When it's firm, remove the cheese from its mold. Sprinkle all sides with salt.

9. Ripen the cheese at 60 degrees Fahrenheit and 90 percent humidity for 3 days or until the whey stops draining. Turn daily and wipe up any whey.

10. Wash the cheese every 2 days using a cloth dipped in brine solution. After 10 to 12 days, an orange smear will appear on the surface. Continue to wash and turn the cheese every other day for at least 2 weeks for 1-pound cheeses, 3 weeks for 2-pound cheeses.

11. Once the rind has developed, wrap the cheese in parchment paper and refrigerate. Authentic Muenster needs about 3 months to ripen, but hold your nose.

Muenster Cheese Soufflé

Yield: 4 servings

Ingredients:

- 1¼ cups whole milk
- 1½ tablespoons butter
- 3 tablespoons all-purpose flour
- ¼ teaspoon ground cumin
- Salt and pepper
- ½ cup fresh breadcrumbs
- 3 large eggs, separated
- 1 cup ½-inch cubes Muenster cheese, aged several months and rindless (*Note:* To cube the Muenster easily, freeze it for 15 minutes.)

1. Bring the milk just to a simmer in a small saucepan, and then remove it from the heat.

2. Melt the butter in a medium saucepan over medium heat. Whisk in the flour.

3. Cook the roux (butter and flour) for 2 minutes, whisking constantly (do not brown). Gradually whisk in the warm milk. Cook until the sauce is smooth and thick enough to drop from the whisk in a thin ribbon, about 7 minutes. Remove from heat.

4. Mix in the cumin and season generously with salt and pepper; transfer the mixture to a glass bowl. Cool for 10 minutes. (This base can be made ahead and refrigerated. Press plastic wrap onto the surface and bring to room temperature before using.)

5. Preheat the oven to 400 degrees Fahrenheit. Butter a 4- to 5-cup soufflé dish, coating the inside with fresh breadcrumbs.

6. Whisk the egg yolks into the soufflé base one at a time; stir in the cheese cubes. Beat the egg whites with a pinch of salt in another bowl until stiff but not dry.

7. Fold the egg whites into the soufflé base in three parts; transfer to the prepared dish.

8. Bake the soufflé until it's puffed, brown on top, and firm but jiggly to the touch, about 25 minutes. Spoon the soufflé onto plates and serve with a tomato salad.

Brick

Brick was invented in Wisconsin around 1877 by John Jossi, a Swiss-born American cheese maker, who wanted a cheese firmer and less overpowering than Limburger—a Limburger "for the spouse who wants to stay married," if you will. This cheese is commercially made in loaf-shaped molds. Not only does it look like a brick, but bricks were originally used to press out whey. Use Brick in your favorite sandwich or in recipes for macaroni and cheese.

Yield: 2 pounds

Ingredients:

✤ 2 gallons pasteurized whole milk

✤ ¼ teaspoon direct-set mesophilic culture or 4 tablespoons mesophilic mother culture

* ⅛ teaspoon *Brevibacterium linens*
* Tiny pinch *Geotrichum candidum*
* ½ teaspoon liquid rennet (or ½ rennet tablet) diluted in ¼ cup unchlorinated water
* Brine bath
* Brine solution for rind washing

1. Use a double boiler or water bath to warm the milk to 90 degrees Fahrenheit.

2. Add the culture, *B. linens,* and *G. candidum*. Let these dissolve on the milk's surface for 5 minutes. Stir gently from bottom to top. Cover and let ripen for 15 minutes.

3. Keeping the milk's temperature at 90 degrees Fahrenheit, add the diluted rennet and stir gently from top to bottom for 1 minute. Cover and let set for 40 minutes or until the curd is firm and separates cleanly.

4. Cut the curd into ½-inch cubes. Let them rest for 10 minutes, and then begin stirring.

5. Gradually raise the temperature to 95 degrees Fahrenheit over about 40 minutes. Do not heat too quickly, and stir gently but often to keep the curd from sticking together. Let rest for 5 minutes.

6. Drain off a third of the whey and replace it with the same amount of water, heated to 104 degrees Fahrenheit, to bring the temperature of the curd to 98 degrees Fahrenheit. Stir gently for 10 minutes.

7. Pour the curd into a cloth-lined colander with a catch bowl beneath it. Fill your mold and cover it to keep the curd warm. Allow the curd to drain for 30 minutes.

8. Flip the mold and continue to let the curd drain for another 30 minutes.

9. Take the cheese out of the mold, peel off the cloth, turn the cheese over, and rewrap it.

10. Press the cheese with a 5-pound weight for 6 hours, turning the cheese every 2 hours.

11. Remove the cheese from the mold and the cloth from the cheese. Place the cheese in a brine bath for 8 hours, turning once after 4 hours. Sprinkle some salt on the cheese's exterior as it soaks.

12. Transfer the cheese from the brine bath to a cheese mat and rack. Pat it dry using a paper towel, and then let it continue drying at room temperature for 24 hours or until it's dry to the touch.

13. Place the cheese in a ripening container to age at 55 to 60 degrees Fahrenheit and 90 to 95 percent humidity for 2 weeks. Flip the cheese daily and wipe the rind every 2 days using a clean cloth or sponge dipped in the brine solution. A reddish smear should appear after 10 to 12 days.

14. After 2 weeks, bacterial growth will turn the rind a more solid reddish brown. Rinse the cheese in cool water and dry it with paper towel. (If you want a stronger flavor, don't rinse the cheese.)

15. Wax or wrap your cheese and age it at 45 degrees Fahrenheit for about 2 months, turning it several times a week.

Raclette

If you've ever been served this melted cheese with boiled new potatoes, gherkins, and pickled onions after a long day on the ski slopes, you'll never forget it. The cheese originated in the Swiss Valais, but the French adopted it. *Racler* means "to scrape," and that's just how it's served at the table, in a luscious golden ribbon. Diners can also melt their own chunks of raclette on a table-top grill in small pans called *coupelles*.

Yield: 2 pounds

Ingredients:

❧ 2 gallons pasteurized whole milk

❧ ¼ teaspoon direct-set mesophilic culture or 4 tablespoons mesophilic mother culture

❧ ⅛ teaspoon *Brevibacterium linens*

❧ Tiny pinch *Geotrichum candidum*

❧ ½ teaspoon liquid rennet (or ½ rennet tablet) diluted in ¼ cup unchlorinated water

❧ Brine bath

❧ Brine solution for rind washing

1. Use a double boiler or water bath to warm the milk to 88 degrees Fahrenheit.

2. Add the culture, *B. linens,* and *G. candidum*. Let them dissolve on the milk's surface for 5 minutes. Stir gently from top to bottom. Cover and let ripen for 1 hour and 15 minutes at 88 degrees Fahrenheit.

3. Add the diluted rennet and stir gently for 1 minute. Cover and let set for 40 minutes or until the curd is firm and separates cleanly.

4. Cut the curd into ¼-inch cubes using a knife and then a whisk. Use a skimmer to lift the curd. Let it rest for 5 minutes.

5. Stir the curd for 20 minutes at 88 degrees Fahrenheit. Let it settle to the bottom of the pot.

6. Using a measuring cup, remove about ¼ of the whey. Replace it with an equal amount of water, heated to 130 degrees Fahrenheit, and stir gently to bring the temperature of the curd to 98 degrees Fahrenheit. Continue to stir for 10 minutes. Let rest.

7. Pour the curd into a cloth-lined colander, fill your mold immediately (so the curd stays warm), and allow it to drain for 20 minutes.

8. Press at light pressure (5 to 10 pounds) for 15 minutes.

9. Remove the cheese from the press and the cloth from the cheese. Turn it over and rewrap it. Press at medium pressure (10 to 20 pounds) for 12 hours or overnight.

10. Transfer the unwrapped cheese to a brine bath for 12 hours, turning once after 6 hours.

11. Remove the cheese from the brine bath, pat it dry, and place it on a cheese mat and rack. Let the cheese dry at room temperature for 24 hours, turning it over several times.

12. Place the cheese in a ripening container to age at 55 to 60 degrees Fahrenheit and 90 to 95 percent humidity to age for 3 days, turning daily.

13. After 3 days, wipe the rind with a clean cloth or sponge dipped in the brine solution. Continue washing the rind and turning the cheese every 2 days for 1 month. A reddish smear will appear.

14. Continue ripening the cheese, turning and wiping it twice a week for 2 months. The brownish rind will grow more pungent as you age it.

Tilsit

Tilsit, or Tilsiter, was originally made in the 1800s by Swiss immigrants in East Prussia, who built their cheese plant in Tilsit, a city in modern-day Russia. Today, it's immensely popular in Switzerland, where you can buy three varieties: mild Tilsit (green label) made from pasteurized milk, stronger Tilsit (red label) made from raw milk, and the most intense Rahm-Tilsiter (yellow label) made from pasteurized milk with added cream.

Like Muenster and Taleggio, Tilsit is not pressed. Instead, it's turned over in its mold and allowed to drain until firm. Perform this trick by holding the mold between two draining mats. Lift it, flip it over, and set it back in the draining pan.

Yield: 2 pounds

Ingredients:

❖ 2 gallons pasteurized whole milk

❖ ¼ teaspoon direct-set thermophilic culture or 4 tablespoons thermophilic mother culture

❖ ⅛ teaspoon *Brevibacterium linens*

❖ Tiny pinch *Geotrichum candidum*

❖ ½ teaspoon liquid rennet (or ½ rennet tablet) diluted in ¼ cup unchlorinated water

❖ Brine bath

❖ Brine solution for rind washing

1. Use a double boiler or water bath to warm the milk to 95 degrees Fahrenheit. Stir gently.

2. Add the culture, *B. linens,* and *G. candidum*. Let them dissolve on the milk's surface for 5 minutes. Stir gently from top to bottom. Cover and let ripen for 30 minutes at 95 degrees Fahrenheit.

3. Add the diluted rennet and stir gently from top to bottom for 1 minute. Cover and let set for 40 minutes or until the curd is firm and separates cleanly.

4. Cut the curd into ½-inch cubes, and then let them rest for 5 minutes.

5. Gradually warm the curd to 110 degrees Fahrenheit over 40 minutes, stirring gently. Do not heat too quickly. The curd should shrink to pea size.

6. Pour off whey to the level of the curd and ladle the warm curd into a mold. Place the mold on a mat in a plastic container. Cover to keep warm.

7. Turn the curd in its mold every 15 minutes for 1 hour, then once every hour for 10 hours or until firm.

8. When the cheese is firm, unwrap it and place it in a brine bath for 12 hours. Turn once after 6 hours.

9. Transfer the cheese from the brine bath to a cheese mat and rack. Let it dry at room temperature for 24 hours, turning it over once.

10. Place the cheese in a ripening container to age at 55 to 60 degrees Fahrenheit and 90 to 95 percent humidity, flipping it daily.

11. After 1 week, wipe the rind twice a week using a clean cloth or sponge dipped in the brine solution. Turn the cheese each time you wash it. A reddish smear should appear.

12. Continue ripening the cheese, turning and wiping it twice a week. For mild flavor, eat after 2 months; for more intense flavor and pungency, wait 6 months.

Taleggio

Taleggio—like Gorgonzola, provolone, mascarpone, and grana padano—comes from Italy's fertile Lombardy region. Unlike cheeses made from lowland cow's milk, Taleggio's buttery texture depends on the high pastures of the Valtellina. Legend has it that milk cows descended from their mountain habitat *stracche* (exhausted).

The soft uncooked curd made from their milk was *stracchino*, another name for Taleggio.

Like Muenster, this cheese is not pressed. Instead, it is turned over in its mold and allowed to drain until firm. Perform this trick by holding the mold between two draining mats. Lift it, flip it over, and set it back in the draining pan. Taleggio is traditionally made in a square mold. When ripe, the cheese should bulge at the sides and be soft, not runny, with a red-brown crust.

Yield: 2 pounds

Ingredients:

❖ 2 gallons pasteurized whole milk

❖ ¼ teaspoon direct-set mesophilic culture or 4 tablespoons mesophilic mother culture

❖ ⅛ teaspoon *Brevibacterium linens*

❖ Tiny pinch *Geotrichum candidum*

❖ ½ teaspoon liquid rennet (or ½ rennet tablet) diluted in ¼ cup unchlorinated water

❖ Brine bath

❖ Brine solution for rind washing

1. Use a double boiler or water bath to warm the milk to 90 degrees Fahrenheit.

2. Add the culture, *B. linens,* and *G. candidum*. Let them dissolve on the milk's surface for 5 minutes. Stir gently from top to bottom. Cover and let ripen for 1 hour at 90 degrees Fahrenheit.

3. Add the diluted rennet and stir gently from top to bottom for 1 minute. Cover and let set for 30 minutes or until the curd is firm and separates cleanly.

4. Cut the curd into 1-inch cubes. Let them rest for 5 minutes, then cut them again into ¼-inch bits using a whisk to cut and a skimmer to lift the curd.

5. Stir the curd for 30 minutes. Every 10 minutes, stop stirring and remove 2 cups of whey

with a measuring cup. Let the curd settle.

6. Gently transfer the soft curd to your mold and allow it to drain for 12 hours. Carefully flip the cheese in its mold every 2 hours, and cover it to keep it warm.

7. When the cheese is firm and has stopped draining, remove it from the mold and unwrap it. Place it in a brine bath for 8 hours, turning once after 4 hours.

8. Transfer the cheese from the brine bath to a cheese mat and rack. Let it dry at room temperature for 2 days, turning several times.

9. Place the cheese in a ripening container to age at 45 degrees Fahrenheit and 90 percent humidity for about 5 weeks. Wash the rind twice a week using a clean cloth or sponge dipped in the brine solution. Washing spreads the bacteria that give Taleggio its red-orange color. The cheese is ripe when it softens and bulges slightly at the sides.

Grilled Cheese and Pear Panini

Yield: 2 sandwiches

Ingredients:

- 1 loaf ciabatta or another rustic Italian bread
- ¼ cup olive oil
- 4 ounces Taleggio, sliced
- 1 large pear, cored and cut into ¼-inch slices
- 1 tablespoon honey
- Pinch salt
- Pinch freshly ground black pepper
- 2 ounces arugula

1. Slice the bread into four pieces for two sandwiches. Brush the slices on both sides with olive oil and place them in a heavy skillet over low heat.

2. While the bread slices are browning, arrange the sandwich filling on top of two of them. Layer the cheese, then the pear slices. Drizzle the pears with honey, and sprinkle them with salt and pepper. Top with arugula leaves. Place the warmed top half of the bread over the arugula.

3. Press down on the sandwiches with the bottom of another skillet (don't crush them).

4. Warm the sandwiches until the cheese melts, and then cut them in half. Serve immediately.

CHAPTER 10

Bloomy Rinds

We have already seen how *Brevibacterium linens* and *Geotrichum candidum* are used to develop the unforgettable odor and taste of washed-rind cheeses in chapter 9. In the next chapters we will see how a variety of bacteria and molds are used to create Camembert's snowy white fuzz and the delectable blue veins of Gorgonzola.

As with the recipes of chapter 9, *B. linens* bacteria can either be added to milk or sprayed on the finished bloomy-rind cheese using an atomizer. In my bloomy-rind recipes, you'll add *Penicillium candidum* during the ripening process for a couple of reasons: it ensures that the mold is evenly distributed throughout the cheese and avoids the unwanted moisture of a surface application.

Bloomy rind describes the edible white fuzz that *P. candidum* helps produce; it's also the nickname for some of the world's favorite cheeses. Brie, in fact, was crowned *roi des fromages* (the king of cheeses) in 1815 at the Congress of Vienna. Today, it's no longer just the privilege of dignitaries and diplomats, but it is still a challenge to make successfully.

Brie, Camembert, and all the other bloomy rinds need 90 percent humidity and an ambient temperature of 50 to 55 degrees Fahrenheit for the mold to grow. Once white mold covers the cheese (about 2 weeks), it's wrapped in double-layer paper and aged for another 4 to 6 weeks. White surface mold ripens the cheese from the outside in, creating a soft paste and a woodsy smell some compare to mushrooms. The texture changes from crumbly to creamy as casein is *hydrolized* (split by water) through enzymatic action. If overripe, these cheeses smell like ammonia—a telltale sign.

> "Essays are writ by fools like me, but only God can make a Brie."
>
> —Clifton Fadiman

MAKING BLOOMY-RIND CHEESES

Mold-ripened cheeses need lots of TLC to ensure they thrive under precise curing conditions. Most home cheese makers who stick with the process say it's worth it. Here are some preparation guidelines.

Pasteurizing your own raw milk may be simpler than you think.

FARM FRESH MILK

With all soft-ripened cheese, if you can get raw milk, pasteurize it yourself by following the steps in chapter 2. If you are sure the milk is clean (and has been tested), try using it unpasteurized for fuller flavor. In that case, add only half as much culture and rennet as the recipe calls for.

DEALING WITH "BAD" MOLD

After draining the cheese, you'll salt it to draw out moisture and retard the growth of organisms you don't want blooming on your cheese. Blue mold, for example, indicates too much moisture, either in the cheese or in the storage container. Reduce the humidity and clean and disinfect the container with bleach water (2 tablespoons bleach to 1 gallon water). Black furry mold (*poil de chat* or *cat's hair*) is also unwelcome. Dab blue or black mold with a solution of 1 teaspoon salt dissolved in ¼ cup vinegar.

AVOIDING CROSS CONTAMINATION

Microorganisms quickly spread from one cheese to another. If you are making only one type of bacteria- and mold-ripened cheese (Brie and Crottin, for example), they can be placed in the same ripening container. Otherwise, put separate cheese types in separate containers (Brie and Gouda, for example).

TRIPLE-CREAM CHEESES

Triple-cream cheeses are luscious and decadent, thanks to the high butterfat content that comes from tripling the cream. They have roughly twice the fat as a typical Brie or Camembert, and they're even more buttery and rich. Some triple-creams are fresh, such as mascarpone; others are soft-ripened, such as Boursault, Brillat-Savarin, Saint André, and Explorateur. Once you've had success with soft-ripened cheeses, experiment with triple-creams by substituting 1 quart of nonhomogenized heavy cream for 1 quart of milk in your favorite recipes.

Bloomy-Rind Cheese Recipes

Like washed-rind cheeses, bloomy-rind cheeses usually aren't pressed. See chapter 9, page 118, for a quick draining how-to.

Camembert

In Vimoutiers, France, the heart of Camembert country, there is a statue of Marie Harel, the woman who, legend says, perfected the recipe for Camembert. She supposedly got the recipe in 1791 in exchange for taking in a homeless friar. What a bargain!

Today, the best French Camembert bears the label "VCN" for *Véritable Camembert de Normandie* as well as the phrase *au lait cru* (made from raw milk). But you'll have to travel to France to buy it. Certified pasteurized versions are illegal for US export because the raw milk is aged less than sixty days. So you'll just have to make your own. Get inspired by tasting a wheel or two from Vermont's Blythedale Farms and New York's Old Chatham Sheepherding Company. Each of these American artisans makes a great Camembert using pasteurized milk.

A word about yield: A half gallon of milk will make enough curd to fill one standard 8-ounce Camembert mold. You will need four molds for a 2-gallon recipe, and eight mats to drain them.

Yield: about 2 pounds

Ingredients:

- ❖ 2 gallons pasteurized whole milk
- ❖ ¼ teaspoon direct-set mesophilic culture or ½ teaspoon Flora Danica (mesophilic aromatic culture)
- ❖ ⅛ teaspoon *Penicillium candidum*
- ❖ Tiny pinch *Geotrichum candidum*
- ❖ ¼ teaspoon liquid rennet (or ¼ rennet tablet) diluted in ¼ cup unchlorinated water
- ❖ 4 teaspoons Kosher salt

Double-Cream Camembert

Not enough butterfat? We can fix that. Add extra richness to this recipe by replacing 2 cups of milk with heavy cream.

1. Use a double boiler or water bath to warm the milk to 85 degrees Fahrenheit, stirring gently.

2. Add the culture, *P. candidum*, and *G. candidum*. Let them dissolve on the milk's surface for 5 minutes, then mix well from top to bottom using a skimmer.

3. Add the diluted rennet and stir gently for 1 minute. Cover and let set at 85 degrees Fahrenheit for 1½ hours or until the curd is firm and separates cleanly.

4. Cut the curd into ½-inch cubes, and let them settle for 5 minutes.

5. Stir and lift the curd very gently using a skimmer for 5 to 10 minutes. Let it settle.

6. Pour off whey to the level of the curd and reserve it for ricotta. Carefully ladle the curd into each sterilized mold. As whey drains, you will need to top off the molds.

7. Set the molds on mats in a draining pan. Every hour for 5 hours, carefully lift the mold between its mats and flip it. Remove any whey. Cover the container and let drain overnight at about 68 degrees Fahrenheit to slow fermentation.

8. Flip the cheeses in the morning and pour off any whey. The cheeses are ready to be removed when they are about 1 to 1½ inches high and have shrunk from the sides of their molds.

9. Sprinkle both sides of the cheeses with salt, and place them on a clean mat in a ripening container. Let the salt dissolve before you cover the container, about 10 minutes.

10. Age the cheeses at 50 to 54 degrees Fahrenheit and 90 percent humidity. Turn the cheeses daily and wipe up any whey that has drained. Excessive moisture will interfere with proper mold growth.

11. After about 1 week, white fuzz will appear. When the white fuzz has fully bloomed and covers each cheese (12 to 14 days), wrap the cheeses in double-layered ripening paper. Let them age another week or until the centers are soft and the sides bulge when brought to room temperature. A ripe Camembert has a pleasing aroma.

Camembert with Calvados

Apple brandy of Normandy, France, marries especially well with this Norman cheese.

Yield: about 6 servings

Ingredients:

❖ 1 wheel (8 ounces) Camembert

❖ 3 tablespoons Calvados (apple brandy)

❖ 1 cup slivered almonds

❖ 1 tablespoon unsalted butter, at room temperature

❖ 2 Granny Smith apples, thinly sliced

❖ Sliced French bread

1. The day before you plan to serve, gently scrape white mold from the cheese surface, but don't remove the rind. Poke the rind lightly all over with a fork. Place the cheese in a pan and pour the Calvados over it. Marinate at room temperature for 24 hours, turning the cheese over occasionally.

2. Combine the butter and almond, and mix well. Pat the nut mixture evenly all over the top and sides of the cheese. Transfer to a baking dish and refrigerate, covered, 1 hour.

3. Preheat the oven to 400 degrees Fahrenheit.

4. Bake the cheese until the nuts are golden brown, about 12 to 15 minutes. Serve at once with the apple slices and French bread.

Brie (Goat's Milk Variation)

This famous cheese has been made in the Brie region, east of Paris, since the fifth century. The best French Brie—name-protected *Brie de Meaux*—is still made there, though dairy cows compete with factories and high-rises. As with Camembert, you won't find any imported Brie made with *lait cru* (raw milk). Instead, look for an AOC (French certification) label if you're shopping for *Brie de Meaux* made with pasteurized milk or sample Blythedale Farm's Vermont Brie.

Whether you're shopping or making your own, it's helpful to know exactly when your soft-ripened cheese is ready to be cut. Remember: once it's cut, it

stops aging. Underripe cheese is chalky and white. Overripe cheese is runny, smells like ammonia, and the rind separates easily from the oozing paste. A truly ripe Brie (à point, as the French say) bulges, it doesn't run, and the paste is straw-colored.

Because recipes for Camembert and Brie are identical (the only difference between these cheeses is the size of their molds), we invite you to try this goat's milk Brie. If you find the paste is too soft, ripen the cheeses at a cooler temperature. This recipe makes five cheeses, 8 ounces each.

Yield: 5 8-ounce cheeses

Ingredients:

- 2 gallons pasteurized goat's milk
- ¼ teaspoon direct-set mesophilic culture or ½ teaspoon Flora Danica (mesophilic aromatic culture)
- ⅛ teaspoon *Penicillium candidum*
- Tiny pinch *Geotrichum candidum*
- ¼ teaspoon liquid rennet (or ¼ rennet tablet) diluted in ¼ cup unchlorinated water
- 4 teaspoons Kosher salt

1. Use a double boiler or water bath to warm the milk to 88 degrees Fahrenheit, stirring gently.

2. Add the culture, *P. candidum*, and *G. candidum*. Let them dissolve on the milk's surface for 5 minutes. Mix well from top to bottom using a skimmer.

3. Add the diluted rennet and stir gently for 1 minute. Cover and let set at 88 degrees Fahrenheit for 1 hour or until the curd is firm and separates cleanly.

4. Cut the curd into 1-inch cubes, and let them settle for 10 minutes.

5. Stir and lift the curd very gently using a skimmer for 5 to 10 minutes, and then let it settle.

6. Pour off whey to the level of the curd. Carefully ladle the curd into each sterilized mold. As the whey drains, top off the mold with more curd.

7. Set the molds on mats in a draining pan. Every hour for 5 hours, carefully lift the mold between its mats and flip it. Remove any whey. Cover the pan and let drain overnight at about 68 degrees Fahrenheit to slow fermentation.

8. Flip the cheeses in the morning and pour off any whey. The cheeses are ready to be removed when they are about 1 to 1½ inches high and have shrunk from the sides of their molds.

9. Sprinkle both sides of the cheeses with salt, and place them on a clean mat in a ripening container. Let the salt dissolve before you cover the container, about 10 minutes.

10. Age the cheeses at 50 to 54 degrees Fahrenheit and 90 percent humidity. Turn the cheeses daily and wipe up any whey that has drained. Excessive moisture will interfere with proper mold growth.

11. After about 1 week, white fuzz will appear. When the white fuzz has fully bloomed and covers each cheese (12 to 14 days), wrap the cheeses in double-layered ripening paper. Let them age 1 to 2 weeks or until the centers are soft and the sides bulge.

Chaource

If Camembert says "Normandy," and Brie, the "Ile-de-France," Chaource is the delectable product of La Champagne (the region) and accompaniment to *le champagne* (the sparkling wine). Named for the town of Chaource, this cheese boasts more butterfat than Brie and is so good that it can be eaten at any stage. Ripeness is more a matter of personal preference. After 2 weeks, it's rather white and chalky; after 1 month, it looks runny and golden and begins to taste fruity; fully aged (up to 2 months), its texture is buttery, its taste sharper, and its crust shows red mottling. French cheese maker Lincet of Saligny sells a pasteurized Chaource. This recipe makes four 8-ounce cheeses or eight 4-ounce cheeses.

Yield: more than 2 pounds

Ingredients:

- ❖ 2 gallons pasteurized whole milk
- ❖ ¼ teaspoon Flora Danica (mesophilic aromatic culture)
- ❖ ⅛ teaspoon *Penicillium candidum*
- ❖ Tiny pinch *Geotrichum candidum*
- ❖ 2 drops liquid rennet, diluted in 5 tablespoons cool unchlorinated water
- ❖ 4 teaspoons Kosher salt

1. Use a double boiler or water bath to warm the milk to 80 degrees Fahrenheit, stirring gently.

2. Add the culture, *P. candidum*, and *G. candidum*. Let them dissolve on the milk's surface for 5 minutes. Mix well from top to bottom using a skimmer.

3. Add the diluted rennet and stir gently for 1 minute. Cover and let set at 80 degrees Fahrenheit for 12 hours or overnight.

4. Remove any whey that's collected on the milk's surface using a measuring cup. Then, using a skimmer, ladle the curd into each sterilized mold. As the whey drains, you will need to top the molds off.

5. Set the molds on mats in a draining pan. Cover them to keep them warm and leave overnight.

6. Carefully lift the molds between two mats and flip them. Remove any whey. The curd should firm up. If it doesn't, wait to flip again. Cover the container and let the cheese drain for another 12 hours. The cheeses are ready to be removed when they have shrunk away from the sides of their molds.

7. Unmold the cheeses, and sprinkle all sides with salt. Place them on clean mats in a clean ripening container, and let the salt dissolve for about 10 minutes before you cover the container.

8. Age the cheeses at 50 to 54 degrees Fahrenheit and 95 percent humidity. Turn the cheeses daily and wipe up any whey that has drained. Excessive moisture will interfere with proper mold growth.

9. After about 1 week, white fuzz should appear. When the white fuzz has fully bloomed and covers each cheese (12 to 14 days), wrap the cheeses in double-layered ripening paper. Longer aging will make a creamier paste and intensify the flavor.

Crottin

Although *crottin de cheval* literally means "horse dung," Crottin cheeses are little barrels of goodness, named for the small French village of Chavignol. The unappetizing name hasn't prevented Crottin's celebrity as the perfect accompaniment to Sancerres wines of the Loire Valley. The cheeses are formed in special 2-by-4-inch molds and are sweet and moist when young; they are brown, hard, and strong when aged more than 2 months. Try them with roasted garlic spread on a French baguette. Another trick is to cut them in half, heat, and serve them on your favorite salad. Redwood Hill Farm makes a splendid California Crottin. You will need about ten Crottin molds for this recipe.

Yield: 1½ pounds

Ingredients:

❖ 1 gallon whole goat's milk

❖ ¼ teaspoon direct-set mesophilic culture or ¼ teaspoon Flora Danica (mesophilic aromatic culture)

❖ Pinch *Penicillium candidum*

❖ Pinch *Geotrichum candidum*

❖ 2 drops liquid rennet diluted in 5 tablespoons cool, unchlorinated water

❖ 4 teaspoons Kosher salt

1. Warm the milk to 72 degrees Fahrenheit. Add the culture, *P. candidum*, and *G. candidum*. Let them dissolve on the milk's surface for 5 minutes. Mix well from top to bottom using a skimmer.

2. Add the diluted rennet and stir gently for 1 minute. Cover and let set at 72 degrees Fahrenheit for 20 hours or until a firm curd forms.

3. Remove any whey that's collected on the milk's surface using a measuring cup. Then, using a skimmer, carefully ladle the curd into each sterilized mold, breaking it as little as possible. Wait until the whey drains, then top the molds off.

4. Set the molds on mats in plastic drainage containers. Cover them to keep them warm and leave them for 24 hours.

5. Carefully lift the molds between their mats and flip them. Remove any whey. The curd should firm up. If it doesn't, wait to flip again. Cover the containers and let them drain another 24 hours. The cheeses are ready to be removed when they have shrunk away from the sides of their molds.

6. Unmold the cheeses, and sprinkle all sides with salt. Return the cheeses to the ripening containers, cover, and continue to let drain for another 24 hours. Remove any collected whey.

7. Place the cheeses on clean mats in clean containers to age at 50 degrees Fahrenheit and 90 percent humidity. Turn the cheeses daily and wipe up any whey that has drained. Excessive moisture will interfere with proper mold growth.

8. After 1 week, white fuzz should appear. When the white fuzz has fully bloomed and covers each cheese (12 to 14 days), wrap the cheeses in double-layered ripening paper and refrigerate them. They are now ready to eat.

Variation: Selles-sur-Cher

Many goat cheeses—Sainte Maure, Valençay, Pouligny-Saint-Pierre—were traditionally dried with ashes, which also encouraged paste ripening. For Selles-sur-Cher, ash is definitive. Make the following changes to the Crottin recipe:

1. Follow steps 1 through 5 of the Crottin recipe.

2. Unmold the cheeses, and sprinkle all sides with salt. Place the cheeses on a paper towel to protect counter surfaces. Use a sieve to dust the cheeses on all sides with vegetable ash (available from cheese-making suppliers). Go for a thin black coating that covers the white surface entirely.

3. Place the cheeses on clean mats in clean containers to age at 50 degrees Fahrenheit and 85 percent humidity. Turn the cheeses daily and wipe up any whey that has drained. Excessive moisture will interfere with proper mold growth.

4. After 2 weeks, wrap the cheeses in double-layered ripening paper and refrigerate them. They are now ready to eat.

CHAPTER 11

Blue Cheese

Blue-veined cheeses are inoculated with a strain of *Penicillium roqueforti* mold, which, when exposed to air, creates a marbled paste and a blue-gray crust. Each country has its own blue cheeses—England's Stilton and Shropshire Blue, Ireland's Cashel Blue, Spain's Cabrales, Italy's Gorgonzola, Germany's Cambozola (a blend of Camembert and Gorgonzola), and, more recently, Denmark's Danish Blue and America's Maytag Blue.

"Majestic Roqueforts looking down with princely contempt upon the others, through the glass of their crystal covers."

—Émile Zola, French writer

And then there's France's Roquefort, aged in the same limestone caves in Cambalou (the Causses region) for over 1,000 years with an unmatched intensity of flavor. French cheese makers still cultivate their blue mold on stale rye bread, harvest it, and either add it to the milk at the start of cheese making or to the curd. As home cheese makers, we can sprinkle in the commercial variety, wait for it to ripen our curd, and wonder again at the miracles of science.

PIERCING THE CHEESE

Blue cheeses are salted to encourage *P. roqueforti* and discourage other molds. After two weeks, the cheeses are pierced with a sterilized knitting needle (the stem of a milk thermometer works well, too) to allow air inside. Here are instructions for piercing your cheeses:

1. Boil the piercing tool in water for several minutes and let cool. (Do not use bleach to sterilize it because bleach may kill the mold.)

2. With your cheese on a flat surface, slowly push the needle right through the cheese, horizontally and vertically, about twenty times.

3. Press down on the cheese lightly when you withdraw the needle so as not to break it.

4. Set the cheese on a clean mat in a clean ripening container. Follow your recipe's directions for ripening.

AGING THE CHEESE

Part of what makes blue cheeses special is that they are difficult to bring to maturity. Like spoiled children, they need what they need, no compromises. If you don't have a cheese cave where you can regulate temperature (between 34 and 60 degrees) and humidity (between 85 to 95 percent), save these recipes until you do.

Blue Cheese Recipes

Like Camembert and Brie, blue cheeses usually aren't pressed. See page 118 in chapter 9 for a quick drainage how-to.

Roquefort

Since the days of Charlemagne, the caves of Cambalou, near the town of Roquefort-sur-Soulzon, have ripened this famous cheese in ideal conditions—cool dampness and constant air flow. Fleurines, currents of air that pass through rock fissures, allow the vaulted caves to breathe. These conditions are ready-made to grow the *P. roqueforti* mold that transforms simple ewe's milk into complex and crumbly Roquefort.

If you're buying imported brands, look for a red sheep label that identifies true French Roquefort. If buying domestic, some American artisanal blues include Rogue Creamery's Rogue River Blue, Willow Hill's Blue Moon, Jasper Hill's Bayley Hazen Blue, Lively Run's Cayuga Blue, Old Chatham's Ewe's Blue and Shaker Blue, and Point Reyes' Original Blue.

P. roqueforti mold can either be added directly to milk, as in these recipes, or sprinkled on the curd as it's draining. Sprinkling the mold on the curd is more traditional, but I prefer adding the mold at the start. You will need a 2-pound tomme mold or four Camembert molds.

Yield: 3 to 4 pounds

Ingredients:

❖ 2 gallons pasteurized sheep's milk

❖ ¼ teaspoon direct-set mesophilic culture or 4 tablespoons mesophilic mother culture

❖ ⅛ teaspoon *Penicillium roqueforti*

❖ ¼ teaspoon liquid rennet, diluted in ¼ cup unchlorinated water

❖ Kosher salt

1. Use a double boiler or water bath to warm the milk to 90 degrees Fahrenheit, stirring gently.

2. Add the *P. roqueforti*, then the culture. Let them dissolve on the milk's surface for 5 minutes. Mix well from top to bottom using a skimmer.

3. Add the diluted rennet and stir gently for 1 minute. Cover and let set at 90 degrees Fahrenheit for 1½ hours or until the curd is firm and separates cleanly.

4. Cut the curd into ½-inch cubes, vertically and horizontally, in a grid pattern. Let them settle for 5 minutes.

5. Pour off whey to the level of the curd. Carefully ladle the curd into a cloth-lined colander with a catch bowl beneath it. Keep the curd warm and let it drain for 30 minutes.

6. Now ladle the curd into the sterilized molds. As the whey drains, you will need to top them off with more curd. Set the molds on a mat in a covered drainage container.

7. Let the curd drain for 2 days at room temperature, flipping the molds every few hours. Wipe up any collected whey.

8. The cheese is ready to be unmolded when it has shrunk from the sides of its mold. Place it on a paper towel. Sprinkle both sides of the cheese with salt, and place it on a clean mat in a ripening container. Don't close the cover for 5 to 7 days to allow the cheese to dry and the air to circulate.

9. Age the cheese at 50 to 54 degrees Fahrenheit and 85 to 90 percent humidity. Turn the cheese daily and wipe up any whey that has drained (excessive moisture will interfere with proper mold growth).

10. After 1 week, pierce the cheese all the way through, horizontally and vertically, per instructions at the start of this chapter. Turn the cheese daily.

11. Blue mold will appear on the cheese in about 10 days. After 2 weeks, pierce the cheese again all over. Continue to ripen it until a blue-gray rind forms. If mold fails to appear, increase the humidity; the cheese is too dry. Too much humidity, however, will encourage too much surface mold. Remove excess surface mold with a solution of 1 tablespoon Kosher salt and ½ cup white vinegar. Pat the rind dry and return the cheese to the container.

12. Age the cheese at least 2 months—longer for saltier, sharper flavor. When the cheese is ready to eat, wrap it in foil or cheese wrap and store it in the fridge.

Roquefort Dressing

Yield: 2 cups

Ingredients:

* 1 cup buttermilk
* 2 to 3 tablespoons mayonnaise or sour cream
* ½ cup crumbled Roquefort
* 2 to 3 tablespoons dried onion flakes
* Salt and pepper to taste
* 1 teaspoon lemon juice

1. In a blender or food processor, mix all ingredients until smooth.
2. Store in a tightly covered jar in the refrigerator until ready to serve.

Waldorf Salad

Use Roquefort dressing in this variation of Waldorf Salad.

Yield: 4 servings

Ingredients:

* 2 tart apples, cut into bite-size pieces
* 2 ripe pears, sliced
* 1 stalk celery, minced or sliced
* ¼ cup raisins
* 2 to 3 tablespoons lemon juice
* ¾ cup chopped toasted walnuts

Combine all salad ingredients and blend well with dressing.

Fourme d'Ambert

A labor of love for farmers in Auvergne, this cow's milk cheese takes its name from the wooden mold (form) used to shape it into a cylinder about 8 inches high and 4 to 5 inches in diameter. Like Stilton, Fourme d'Ambert is lightly pressed and name-controlled. It is a pretty sight on a cheese platter with its marbled white interior and gray-brown crust. Enjoy this blue with the big French reds—Burgundy, Bordeaux, and Beaujolais. You will need a 2-pound tomme mold for this recipe.

Yield: about 2 pounds

Ingredients:

- ❧ 2 gallons pasteurized whole milk
- ❧ ¼ teaspoon direct-set mesophilic culture or 4 tablespoons mesophilic mother culture
- ❧ ⅛ teaspoon *Penicillium roqueforti*
- ❧ ¼ teaspoon liquid rennet, diluted in ¼ cup unchlorinated water
- ❧ Brine bath (see chapter 6, page 76)

1. Use a double-boiler or water bath to warm the milk to 90 degrees Fahrenheit, stirring gently.

2. Add the *P. roqueforti*, and then add the culture. Let them dissolve on the milk's surface for 5 minutes. Mix well from top to bottom using a skimmer.

3. Add the diluted rennet and stir gently for 1 minute. Cover and let set at 90 degrees Fahrenheit for 1½ hours or until the curd is firm and separates cleanly.

4. Cut the curd into ½-inch cubes, vertically and horizontally, in a grid pattern. Let them settle for 5 minutes.

5. Gently stir curd for 1 hour until the pieces shrink and firm up.

6. Pour off the whey to the level of the curd. Ladle curd into a sterilized, cloth-lined tomme mold. As the whey drains, you will need to top off the curd.

7. Place the mold in your cheese press and apply light pressure (5 to 10 pounds) for 1 hour. Remove the cheese from the press and the cloth from the cheese. Turn it over and rewrap it. Continue light pressure for 6 hours.

8. Remove the cheese from the press, unwrap it, and put it in a brine bath for 12 hours. Flip the cheese after 6 hours.

9. Dry the cheese on a rack for 2 days at room temperature. Pierce all the way through, horizontally and vertically, using a sterilized needle or another tool.

10. Place the cheese on a clean mat in a ripening container. Age at 50 degrees Fahrenheit and 90 percent humidity. Turn the cheese daily and wipe up any whey that has drained (excessive moisture will interfere with proper mold growth).

11. After 1 week, pierce the cheese all the way through, horizontally and vertically, per the instructions on page 138. This allows oxygen to reach the cheese center and facilitates veining of the mold. Turn the cheese daily.

12. After 2 weeks, a bluish moldy crust will begin to form. Continue to ripen for 1 month, at which time it's ready to eat. Wrap it and store it in the fridge.

Stilton

The pride of Britain—and its only name-protected cheese—boasts a mellow creaminess that nicely balances its acidic blue veining. In England, Stilton is sold in 16-pound cylinders, and a trick called *ironing* is used to tell whether the wheel is ready to eat. The cheese maker withdraws a plug of cheese using a cheese trier, sniffs it, examines it, tastes it, and then replaces it. The scar that remains is actually proof that the Stilton got the proper care. Stilton weighs in with a fat content of 55 percent. You can use a 2-pound tomme mold to make this recipe.

Yield: about 2 pounds

Ingredients:

❖ 2 gallons pasteurized whole milk

❖ 2 cups whipping cream (at least 35 percent milk fat)

❖ ¼ teaspoon direct-set mesophilic culture or 4 tablespoons mesophilic mother culture

❖ ⅛ teaspoon *Penicillium roqueforti*

❖ ¼ teaspoon liquid rennet, diluted in ¼ cup unchlorinated water

❖ 2 tablespoons Kosher salt

1. In a double boiler or water bath, warm the milk and cream to 86 degrees Fahrenheit, stirring gently.

2. Add the *P. roqueforti*, then the culture. Let them dissolve on the milk's surface for 5 minutes. Mix them well from top to bottom using a skimmer. Cover and let ripen for 1 hour.

3. Add the diluted rennet and stir gently for 1 minute. Cover and let set at 86 degrees Fahrenheit for 1½ hours or until the curd is firm and separates cleanly.

4. Use the skimmer to ladle slices of the curd into a cloth-lined colander. Place the colander in a catch bowl so that the curd will sit in its own whey. Put the catch bowl in a water bath and maintain it at 86 degrees Fahrenheit. Cover the colander and let the curd drain for 1½ hours. After 45 minutes, break up the curd and turn it to help it firm up.

5. Tie the corners of the muslin holding the curd. Suspend the bag and let it drain till the liquid stops running.

6. When the curd stops dripping, place the bag on a board where it can easily drain. Put a board on top and an 8- to 10-pound weight on top of the board. (A filled gallon jug of water weighs 8 pounds.) Press overnight at room temperature.

7. Remove the curd from the bag, break it up with your fingers (mill it), and add the salt. Fill a sterilized

2-pound mold with the salted curd.

8. Put the mold on a clean mat in a drainage container with a mat on top. Carefully flip the mold every 15 minutes for the next 2 hours. Let the curd drain overnight. Flip it several times a day for the next 4 days, wiping up any whey.

9. When the cheese holds its shape, remove it from the mold. Use a sterilized needle or another tool to pierce it all the way through, horizontally and vertically, per the instructions on page 138.

10. Age the cheese at 50 to 55 degrees Fahrenheit and 90 percent humidity for 4 months. During the first week, turn the cheese daily and wipe the rind with a cloth soaked in brine. Remove any liquid from the ripening container. Turn the cheese several times a week until it's ready to eat. Then wrap it in foil or cheese wrap and store it in the fridge.

Gorgonzola

Like Roquefort, Gorgonzola was originally cured in caves—caves of the Valsassina Valley near Milan. While Roquefort—made with sheep's milk—is crumbly and salty, Lombardy's most famous cheese—made with cow's milk—is creamy and sweet. Gorgonzola *dolce* is the familiar version, aged 6 months. A sharper, *piccante* version is aged at least a year and is washed with brine to encourage the growth of surface bacteria and a powerful aroma.

Fortunately, there are excellent imported brands of Gorgonzola to inspire any cheese hobbyist. If you're curious to know what American artisans have invented, try Rogue Creamery's Oregonzola (and their other amazing blues), BelGioioso Creamy Gorgonzola, and Great Hill Blue. Great Hill Blue is made with raw cow's milk and aged 4 to 6 months.

Traditionally, Gorgonzola cheese makers combined two batches of curd—one from the evening's milk, one from the morning's milk. The village of Gorgonzola was a stopover for herdsmen bringing cows up and down the Alps. *Stracca* means "tired" in Italian, which is what these cows were—tired, and full of milk. *Stracchino di Gorgonzola* (stracchino cheese of Gorgonzola) is the result of an abundance of milk.

The two layers of curd don't blend perfectly, allowing blue mold to thrive and radiate throughout the paste. My recipe uses this layering process: the measurements are for one batch of cheese, which you'll make twice.

Yield: more than 2 pounds

Ingredients:

- ❖ 2 gallons pasteurized whole milk
- ❖ ¼ teaspoon direct-set mesophilic culture or 4 tablespoons mesophilic mother culture
- ❖ Pinch *Penicillium roqueforti*
- ❖ ½ teaspoon liquid rennet (or ½ rennet tablet) diluted in ¼ cup unchlorinated water
- ❖ 2 tablespoons Kosher salt

1. Use a double boiler or water bath to warm the milk to 86 degrees Fahrenheit, stirring gently.

2. Add the *P. roqueforti*, then the culture. Let them dissolve on the milk's surface for 5 minutes. Mix well from top to bottom using a skimmer. Let ripen for 30 minutes.

3. Add the diluted rennet and stir gently for 1 minute. Cover and let set at 86 degrees Fahrenheit for 45 minutes or until the curd is firm and separates cleanly.

4. Cut the curd into ½-inch cubes, vertically and horizontally, in a grid pattern. Let the cubes settle for 10 minutes.

5. Pour off whey to the level of the curd. Gently spoon curd into a cloth-lined colander. Tie the corners of the muslin together, and hang the bag to drain overnight in a cool room (about 60 degrees Fahrenheit).

6. In the morning, make a second batch of curd following steps 1 through 5. Drain the new bag of curd for 1 hour.

7. After 1 hour, cut or break the new curd into 1-inch chunks, and place them in a bowl. Cut the old curd into 1-inch chunks and put them in a separate bowl. Mix 2 tablespoons of salt into each batch.

8. Fill a sterilized, 2-pound mold with cheese chunks, placing the new warm curd on the bottom and sides and the older curd in the center. Top with warm curd from the second batch. Pull the cloth tight and fold it over the top.

9. Press with 5 pounds of pressure in a cool room (about 60 degrees Fahrenheit) for 10 hours. Unwrap the cheese every 2 hours and flip it. Rewrap it and continue pressing.

10. When the cheese is firm, remove it from the mold and sprinkle it with salt on all sides. If it's still soft, let it continue to drain in its mold. Put the cheese on a clean mat in a ripening container and age at 55 degrees Fahrenheit and 85 percent humidity for 4 days. Rub the cheese with salt each day as you turn it. Wipe up any collected whey (excess moisture will prevent proper mold growth).

11. Turn the cheese daily for another 2 weeks. Then pierce it all the way through, horizontally and

vertically, using a sterilized needle or another tool, per the instructions on page 138.

12. After 1 month, pierce the cheese again. Increase the humidity to 90 percent, decrease the temperature to 50 degrees Fahrenheit, and continue to age the cheese for another 2 months. Every few days, scrape mold off the cheese's surface using a knife, and wipe it clean with a cloth dipped in brine. You can eat the cheese after 6 months for *dolce* or up to a year for *piccante*.

Chicken à la Gorgonzola

Yield: 6 servings

Ingredients:

- 3 large chicken breasts, skinned, boned, and halved lengthwise
- 2 tablespoons onion, finely chopped
- ¼ cup butter
- 1 pound fresh baby spinach, blanched, drained, and chopped (or 1 10-ounce package frozen, chopped spinach, thawed and drained)
- ½ cup fresh breadcrumbs
- 4 ounces Gorgonzola, crumbled
- 2 teaspoons lemon juice
- 3 tablespoons flour
- ¾ cup chicken broth or bouillon
- ¼ cup dry white wine
- Salt and pepper
- Paprika

1. Pound the chicken to ¼-inch thickness.

2. Sauté the onion in 2 tablespoons butter until it's tender. Add the spinach; cook it just to remove the moisture. Add the crumbs, cheese, and lemon juice.

3. Put ¼ cup of the mixture on each chicken piece. Fold in the sides of the chicken, roll it, and skewer or tie it. Coat the chicken in flour and brown it in the remaining butter.

4. Preheat the oven to 325 degrees Fahrenheit.

5. Place the chicken in a baking dish. Add the broth and wine, plus salt and pepper to taste, to the drippings in the skillet. Heat the sauce and pour it over the chicken. Cover the chicken and bake it in the oven for 30 minutes.

6. Uncover the chicken and sprinkle it with paprika. Bake it for another 10 to 15 minutes. Remove the chicken to a platter, and stir the remaining juice in the pan to blend it. Thicken it, if necessary, with 1 teaspoon flour mixed with 1 tablespoon water. Serve the gravy over the chicken.

CHAPTER 12

Hard Cheese

"Early in life I learned to see the beauty of great slabs or rounds of cheese on the table."

—James Beard

What kitchen doesn't have a cheese grater for shaving aromatic hunks of Parmesan or Romano? However, we would be robbing our taste buds to reserve these aged beauties only for pasta or casserole toppings. Hard Italian cheeses used for grating are also delicious when served as appetizers or with dessert. These curds are cooked slowly at high heat, cut to the size of lentils, and pressed into huge wheels. Lack of moisture allows them to ripen and develop flavor for years without spoiling.

Gruyère is included here, although it's made with whole milk, not with the low-fat milk of Parmesan and Montasio. Some prefer the French Gruyère called *Comté*, with the "eyes" of genuine Swiss cheese, or the creamier Beaufort, often considered the prince of Gruyère. Whatever your preference, whether you serve them as fondue or with fresh fruit, these versatile cheeses deserve respect. Many hard cheeses can be eaten after six months, but longer aging intensifies their flavor and aroma.

Removing Mold

Unlike with mold-ripened cheese, we want to encourage dryness and inhibit mold growth as we age hard cheeses. If mold appears on the rind, wipe it off using a solution of 1 tablespoon Kosher salt in ½ cup white vinegar.

Hard Cheese Recipes

For all hard cheese, increase the heat when recipes call for it no more than 2 degrees every 5 minutes. Several of these recipes require that you soak the cheese in a brine bath (see chapter 6, page 76 for instructions).

Parmesan

Parmigiano-Reggiano (Parmesan, for short) is considered a *grana*, Italian for "hard cheese with grainy texture." Grana cheeses can be grated for cooking or eaten at the table. As northern Italy's most celebrated cheese, Parmesan's production is strictly controlled—by season, location, size of wheel, type of milk used, and so on. If you were to examine a typical 66-pound wheel, you'd see the date of production, season, and location stamped on its golden rind. Parmesan is usually aged two years; three-year-old Parmesan is called *stravecchio* (very old) and four-year-old Parmesan is called *stravecchione* (extremely old). Longer aging produces complex, melt-in-your-mouth flavor.

Parma and Reggio, two of eight provinces in the Emilia-Romagna region, lay claim to this world-class cheese. Parma is as famous for its ham as it is for its cheese. How did those hogs get so healthy? By slurping whey left over from cheese making, of course. And because true Parmesan is always made with partially skimmed milk, we, too, can afford to be piggy and consume its 28 to 32 percent fat content.

Any cheese monger will tell you that cutting a giant wheel of Parmesan is an art. The ritual requires three special knives—one for scoring the rind, one for piercing the cheese, and one to pry apart the wedge of cheese. Speaking of cutting, never buy your Parmesan already cut or grated. This is a costly cheese; you'll want to consume it as fresh as possible. A less costly import is grana padano, or try Wisconsin-made SarVecchio Parmesan.

Yield: 1½ pounds

Ingredients:

❖ 2 gallons partially skimmed cow's milk (2 percent)

❖ ¼ teaspoon direct-set thermophilic culture or 4 tablespoons thermophilic mother culture

❖ ¼ teaspoon lipase powder, dissolved in ¼ cup cool unchlorinated water and allowed to set for 20 minutes (optional, for stronger flavor)

❖ ½ teaspoon liquid rennet (or ½ rennet tablet) diluted in ¼ cup cool unchlorinated water

❖ Brine bath

❖ Olive oil

1. In a double boiler or water bath, warm the milk to 92 degrees Fahrenheit, stirring gently.

2. Add the culture and lipase powder. Let them dissolve on the milk's surface for 2 minutes, then stir well using an up-and-down motion. Cover and let ripen for 40 minutes at 92 degrees Fahrenheit.

3. Add the diluted rennet and stir gently from top to bottom for 1 minute. Cover and let set at 92 degrees Fahrenheit for 30 minutes or until the curd gives a clean break.

4. Cut the curd into lentil-size pieces using a whisk to slice and a skimmer to lift up and move the curd. Make sure all the curd is cut; then let it settle for 10 minutes.

5. Slowly raise the milk's temperature to 124 degrees Fahrenheit, stirring continuously to prevent matting. Do not heat too quickly; this should take no less than 1 hour. Curd pieces will shrink to the size of rice grains. With the temperature at 124 degrees Fahrenheit, let the curd settle for 5 minutes.

6. Pour the curd and whey into a muslin-lined colander. Let it drain for 5 minutes.

7. Line a 2-pound tomme mold with muslin and place the curd in it. Press at light pressure (5 to 10 pounds) for 1 hour.

8. Remove the cheese from the press and the cloth from the cheese. Turn over the cheese, rewrap it, and press it at medium pressure (10 to 20 pounds) for 2 hours. Repeat this process, turning the cheese and increasing the pressure slightly. End by pressing with firm pressure (20 to 45 pounds) overnight.

9. Take the cheese from the press, unwrap it, and soak it in a brine bath for 20 hours, turning the cheese once.

10. Transfer the cheese from the brine bath to a clean mat. Air-dry it at room temperature for 2 to 3 days, turning it every 6 hours.

11. When the cheese is dry to your touch, let it cure at 50 degrees Fahrenheit and 85 percent humidity for 6 months. Turn it daily, then weekly after 1 month. If mold appears, rub the rind with a vinegar-salt solution. After 3 months, rub the surface with olive oil to seal in moisture and nurture a smooth rind. If the rind looks like it's drying out, rub it with olive oil. Parmesan is ready to eat after 10 months, but longer aging means more intense flavor.

Parmesan-Artichoke Risotto

Cooking baby artichokes with rice creates a risotto infused with the flavor of this delicate vegetable.

Yield: 6 servings

Ingredients:

- 5½ cups (or more) chicken broth, low-sodium or homemade
- 2 tablespoons butter
- 2 tablespoons extra virgin olive oil
- 1 cup finely chopped medium onion
- 8 baby artichokes, trimmed and cut lengthwise
- 1½ cups (about 10 ounces) arborio rice
- ½ cup dry white wine
- ½ cup finely grated Parmesan cheese
- Salt and pepper

1. Bring the broth to a simmer, then remove it from heat and cover the pan to keep it warm.

2. Melt the butter with the oil in a heavy pot over medium-high heat. Add the onion and sauté it until it's soft and golden, about 5 minutes.

3. Add the artichokes. Cover and cook until they begin to brown, stirring often, about 6 minutes.

4. Add the rice and stir for 2 minutes. Add the wine and stir until it's absorbed, about 1 minute.

5. Add 1½ cups warm broth and cook until it's absorbed, stirring often, about 5 minutes. Add more broth, ½ a cupful at a time, allowing each addition to be absorbed before adding the next and stirring often, until the rice is just tender and the mixture is creamy, about 20 minutes longer.

6. Remove the pot from heat, and stir in the cheese. Season it with salt and pepper to taste. Transfer the mixture to a bowl and serve.

Pecorino Romano

Pecorino means "sheep's milk cheese" and *Romano* means "Roman." But few companies make this sharp grana cheese in Rome; the majority comes from Sardinia, where sheep still outnumber residents. Still, the cheese is called Romano, and it is as essential to the southern Italian diet as Parmigiano-Reggiano is to the northern Italian diet.

Name-controlled Pecorino Romano has its own special rituals: the curd is "rummaged" to promote whey drainage and pierced with needles to allow salt penetration. It's always aged at least 8 months. If

you are lucky enough to source 2 gallons of sheep's milk, remember that your yield will be about 4 pounds of cheese because of high milk solids. Not so lucky? Substitute 1 gallon of cow's milk and 1 gallon of goat's milk in this recipe.

Yield: 3 to 4 pounds

Ingredients:

❖ 2 gallons sheep's milk or 1 gallon each cow's and goat's milk (*Note*: this substitution will result in a lower yield.)

❖ ¼ teaspoon direct-set thermophilic culture or 4 tablespoons thermophilic mother culture

❖ ¼ teaspoon liquid rennet (or ¼ rennet tablet) diluted in ¼ cup cool unchlorinated water

❖ Brine bath

❖ Olive oil

1. In a double boiler or water bath, warm the milk to 90 degrees Fahrenheit, stirring gently.

2. Add the culture, let it dissolve on the milk's surface for 2 minutes, then stir well using an up-and-down motion. Cover and let ripen for 15 minutes at 90 degrees Fahrenheit.

3. Add the diluted rennet and stir gently from top to bottom for 1 minute. Cover and let set at 90 degrees Fahrenheit for 45 minutes or until the curd gives a clean break.

4. Cut the curd into ¼-inch pieces using a whisk to slice and a skimmer to lift up and move the curd. Make sure all the curd is cut.

5. Slowly raise the milk's temperature to 118 degrees Fahrenheit, stirring continuously to prevent matting. This should take no less than 50 minutes. With the temperature at 118 degrees Fahrenheit, cover the pot and let the curd settle for 30 minutes.

6. Pour the curd and whey into a muslin-lined colander. Let it drain for 5 minutes.

7. Line a 2-pound tomme mold with muslin and pile the curd in it. Press at light pressure (5 to 10 pounds) for 30 minutes.

8. Remove the cheese from the press and the cloth from the cheese. Turn over the cheese, rewrap it, and press it at medium pressure (10 to 20 pounds) for 3 hours. Repeat this process several times, finally pressing at firm pressure (20 to 45 pounds) for 12 hours or overnight.

9. Take the cheese from the press, unwrap it, and soak it in a brine bath for 20 hours, turning the cheese once.

10. Transfer the cheese from the brine bath to a clean mat. Air-dry it at room temperature for 2 to 3 days, turning it every 6 hours.

11. When the cheese is dry to your touch, let it cure at 55 degrees Fahrenheit and 85 percent humidity for at least 5 months. Turn it daily, then weekly after 1 month. If mold appears, rub the rind with a vinegar-salt solution. After 3 months, rub the surface with olive oil to seal in moisture and nurture a smooth rind. If the rind looks like it's drying out, rub with olive oil as necessary. Pecorino Romano is ready to eat after 8 months, but a 2-year-old cheese will boast more bite.

Swiss Gruyère

You've tasted this cheese melted—in fondues, soufflés, onion soup, and omelets—but Gruyère's dense, meaty flavor makes it a yummy table cheese any way you slice it. Some say it tastes of Alpine air and the sweet grasses and aromatic flowers that fatten grazing cattle there. High-pasture cattle are known for producing milk that's higher in butterfat than lowland cattle produce.

Not surprisingly for such a popular cheese, the French and Swiss both claim inventing it. Its birthplace may have been the town of Gruyères in Switzerland's canton of Fribourg. In fact, Fribourg is the name of a sharp, dry Gruyère that's aged at least two years. But *gruyere* is also an ancient French word meaning "forests." In Alpine regions, cheese makers needed wood from these forests to cook their curd and often paid for it with cheeses. The name *Gruyere* may have taken on a double meaning—forests and the cheese made in them.

Swiss Gruyère sells in 65- to 85-pound wheels and is best cut from the wheel rather than bought pre-cut. Roth Käse USA in Monroe, Wisconsin, makes an 18-pound Gruyère worth seeking out.

Yield: 2 pounds

Ingredients:

❧ 2 gallons pasteurized whole milk

❧ ¼ teaspoon direct-set thermophilic culture or 4 tablespoons thermophilic mother culture

❧ ½ teaspoon liquid rennet (or ½ rennet tablet) diluted in ¼ cup cool unchlorinated water

❧ Brine bath

1. In a double boiler or water bath, warm the milk to 90 degrees Fahrenheit, stirring gently.

2. Add the culture, let it dissolve on the milk's surface for 2 minutes, then stir well using an up-and-down motion. Cover and let ripen for 15 minutes at 90 degrees Fahrenheit.

3. Add the diluted rennet and stir gently from top to bottom for 1 minute. Cover and let set at 90 degrees Fahrenheit for 40 minutes or until the curd gives a clean break.

4. Cut the curd into tiny pieces using a whisk to slice and a skimmer to lift up and move the curd. Make sure all the curd is cut.

5. Slowly raise the milk temperature to 120 degrees Fahrenheit, stirring continuously to prevent matting. This should take no less than 1 hour. With the temperature at 120 degrees Fahrenheit, let the curd settle for 5 minutes.

6. Pour the curd and whey into a muslin-lined colander. Let it drain for 5 minutes.

7. Line a 2-pound tomme mold with muslin and place the curd in it. Press it at light pressure (5 to 10 pounds) for 1 hour.

8. Remove the cheese from the press and the cloth from the cheese. Turn over the cheese, rewrap it, and press it at medium pressure (10 to 20 pounds) for 3 hours. Repeat this process, turning the cheese and raising the pressure slightly. End by pressing at firm pressure (20 to 45 pounds) overnight.

9. Take the cheese from the press, unwrap it, and soak it in a brine bath for 12 hours, turning the cheese once.

10. Transfer the cheese from the brine bath to a clean mat. Air-dry it at room temperature for 2 to 3 days, turning it every 6 hours.

11. When the cheese is dry to your touch, you can either wax it or let it ripen faster with a natural rind. For a natural rind, rub it with a vinegar-salt solution twice a week for the first month, then weekly, to inhibit mold. A natural rind needs about 90 percent humidity and 55 degrees Fahrenheit; waxed cheese can age at 85 percent humidity and 55 degrees Fahrenheit. Turn the cheese daily, then weekly after 1 month. Natural-rind Gruyère will be ready to eat in 6 months; allow waxed Gruyère at least 10 months. For nutty yet delicate flavor, let it cure 1 year.

Three-Cheese Fondue

Each of these Swiss cheeses adds to a memorable meal, traditionally melted in an earthenware pot and accompanied by beer or kirsch.

Ingredients:

- 1½ cups Gruyère, cut in tiny cubes
- 1½ cups Emmental, cut in tiny cubes
- ½ cup Appenzeller, cut in tiny cubes
- 2 to 3 tablespoons cornstarch or all-purpose flour
- 1 clove garlic
- 1 cup dry white wine
- 1 teaspoon lemon juice
- Nutmeg and black pepper
- Crusty bread, cut into cubes

1. Combine the 3 cheeses and cornstarch in a medium-size bowl.
2. Rub the garlic on the inside of a fondue pot; then add the wine and heat until nearly boiling. Stir in the lemon juice.
3. Add a handful of cheese at a time to the hot wine mixture, stirring constantly. Wait until the cheese is melted before adding more.
4. Continue stirring until the mixture is bubbling gently and looks like a creamy sauce. Season with pepper and nutmeg to taste.
5. Remove the pot from the stove and place over a safety burner, adjusted so that the fondue continues to bubble gently. Serve with fondue forks and chunks of bread.

Montasio

Another Alpine cheese, this one dates back to the thirteenth century, when it was created by monks on a pasture-terraced mountain called Montasio. Montasio is a cousin to Asiago and a twin to Carnia, produced in the same Friuli-Venezia Giulia region of Italy. In 1986, it was awarded *denominazione di origine controllata* (DOC) status, meaning "controlled designation of origin." Look for the label as a guarantee of authenticity. As with Parmesan, aged Montasio can be grated and younger cheese enjoyed with fresh pears, prosciutto di Parma, and a glass of fruity Friuli red.

The Mozzarella Company, in Dallas, Texas, makes an interesting Montasio with rosemary and whole cow's milk. Traditionally, this cheese is made, like Parmesan, with partially skimmed milk. My recipe calls for a blend of cow's and goat's milk.

Yield: 2 pounds

Ingredients:

❖ 1 gallon pasteurized cow's milk

❖ 1 gallon pasteurized goat's milk

❖ ¼ teaspoon direct-set thermophilic culture or 4 tablespoons thermophilic mother culture

❖ ½ teaspoon liquid rennet (or ½ rennet tablet) diluted in ¼ cup cool unchlorinated water

❖ Brine bath

❖ Olive oil

1. In a double boiler or water bath, warm the milk to 95 degrees Fahrenheit, stirring gently.

2. Add the culture, let it dissolve on the milk's surface for 2 minutes, then stir well using an up-and-down

motion. Cover and let ripen for 30 minutes at 95 degrees Fahrenheit.

3. Add the diluted rennet and stir gently from top to bottom for 1 minute. Cover and let set at 95 degrees Fahrenheit for 30 minutes or until the curd gives a clean break.

4. Cut the curd into pea-size pieces, using a whisk to slice and a skimmer to lift up and move the curd. Make sure all the curd is cut, and then let it rest for 5 minutes.

5. Slowly raise the milk's temperature to 110 degrees Fahrenheit, stirring continuously to prevent matting. This should take no less than 30 minutes. With the temperature at 110 degrees Fahrenheit, keep stirring for 30 minutes. Let settle for 5 minutes.

6. Pour the curd and whey into a muslin-lined colander. Let it drain for 5 minutes.

7. Line a 2-pound tomme mold with muslin and place the curd in it. Press it at light pressure (5 to 10 pounds) for 1 hour.

8. Remove the cheese from the press and the cloth from the cheese. Turn over the cheese, rewrap it, and press it at medium pressure (10 to 20 pounds) for 3 hours. Repeat this process, turning the cheese and raising the pressure slightly. End by pressing it at firm pressure (20 to 45 pounds) overnight.

9. Take the cheese from the press, unwrap it, and soak it in a brine bath for 12 hours, turning the cheese once.

10. Transfer the cheese from the brine bath to a clean mat. Air-dry it at room temperature for 2 to 3 days, turning it every 6 hours.

11. When the cheese is dry to your touch, let it cure at 55 degrees Fahrenheit and 85 percent humidity. Turn it daily, then weekly after 1 month. If mold appears, rub the rind with a vinegar-salt solution. After 2 months, rub the surface with olive oil to seal in moisture and nurture a smooth rind. If the rind looks like it's drying out, rub it with olive oil as necessary. Montasio is ready to eat after 6 months, but longer curing yields a sharper-tasting cheese.

Cheese Puffs (Gougères)

Parmesan can be substituted for Montasio in this classic recipe that makes a great party snack or appetizer.

Yield: 2 dozen gougères

Ingredients:

❖ 1 cup all-purpose flour

❖ ½ teaspoon salt

❖ ½ teaspoon black pepper

❖ ½ teaspoon thyme

- ❖ Pinch cayenne pepper
- ❖ 1 cup whole milk
- ❖ 4 ounces unsalted butter, cut into ½-inch cubes
- ❖ 5 extra large eggs, at room temperature
- ❖ ¾ cup Montasio cheese, freshly grated
- ❖ ½ cup Gruyère cheese, freshly grated

1. Preheat the oven to 400 degrees Fahrenheit. In a medium bowl, combine the flour, salt, black pepper, thyme, and cayene. Set aside.
2. In a large saucepan, combine the milk and butter and bring it to a boil over high heat.
3. When the butter melts, turn off the heat and add the seasoned flour all at once. With a wooden spoon, stir vigorously just until the dough masses into a ball and does not cling to the sides of the pan.
4. Transfer the dough to a large mixing bowl. On medium speed, beat in 4 of the eggs, one at a time. Stir after each addition until the egg is completely absorbed. The dough should be smooth and satiny.
5. Add the Montasio and Gruyère cheeses to the dough and mix thoroughly.
6. Spoon the dough, 1 large tablespoon at a time, onto buttered baking sheets. Separate the gougères by 1½ inches.
7. Beat the remaining egg and, using a pastry brush, lightly brush the gougères to glaze them.
8. Bake for 10 to 15 minutes until the gougères are golden brown. Let them cool slightly and serve.

CHAPTER 13

Serving Your Cheese

Now that you are a cheese hedonist (one who delights in the sensual pleasures of cheese), you'll want to share that love with friends. In this chapter, we'll begin with the basic rules for serving cheese, followed by some creative ideas for cheese pairings to make your cheese board fun and festive. First, a word about tasting cheese with the eyes, nose, and mouth.

HOW TO TASTE CHEESE

If you've ever been to a wine tasting, you know the importance of smell. Younger wines have *aroma*, older wines *bouquet*. Our palates are limited tasting tools, but our noses register complex flavors long after we've swallowed what we ate or drank. Like wine, cheeses also have eye appeal. Does the rind contrast with the paste? Is the paste runny, crumbly, or flaky? Does the color and texture vary? You will want to present your cheeses to highlight their most appetizing and unusual qualities.

> "A dessert without cheese is like a beautiful woman with only one eye."
>
> —Jean-Anthelme Brillat-Savarin

HOW TO SERVE CHEESE

A bit of serving etiquette will help you display and enjoy the best qualities of your artisan cheeses.

❖ Bring cheese to room temperature (about 72 degrees Fahrenheit) before offering it to guests. Temperature affects cheese flavor and aroma. Allow two to three hours for your cheese to warm up, and keep it wrapped while it's warming.

❖ Trim off any dry edges or surface mold.

❖ Lay out your cheeses on a sturdy wooden or marble platter. Allow enough room for your guests to cut them and help themselves.

❖ Choose no more than six cheeses so that your guests can concentrate on their flavors.

❖ Allow about 4 ounces of cheese per person if the cheese is a dessert or an appetizer, 6 ounces if it's the main course.

❖ Cut soft cheeses while they are still cold and any hard cheese your guests might have difficulty cutting themselves. Provide one utensil for each cheese so that the flavors don't mix. Use a cheese shaver or plane for hard cheese, a cheese knife with two prongs at the tip for slicing and spearing soft cheese, wire slicers for semi-hard cheese, and a spoon for runny cheese. Remember that your guests want to taste the prize—not wear it on their shirts.

❖ Refrigerate leftover cheese as soon as possible.

HOW TO SELECT CHEESE

Balance is key to a memorable tasting. For example, a tangy Gorgonzola, a mild Brie, and a hearty Cheddar will marry well—on the platter and on the tongue. A smoked cheese will overwhelm almost every other type, so use it sparingly. Here are a few ways that you can select your cheeses.

By texture. Select cheese with a variety of textures. You might combine a fresh cheese such as feta with a semi-hard Gruyère and a hard aged Parmesan.

By versions of the same cheese. Choose different types of Camembert or blue cheese, for example, that are produced in entirely different regions of the country. In this case, it's important to label each product. To sample them in one sitting is an education.

By types of milk. You can assemble a cheese platter by choosing cheeses made from cow's, goat's, sheep's, or buffalo's milk. At most, choose two of each kind. The variety will surprise your guests.

By local producers. Experiment by serving only locally made cheeses, and pair them with locally made wines and beers. It's a great way to boost your region's economy while gaining an appreciation for your community.

ACCOMPANIMENTS

Bread and crackers are a good match as long as their flavors don't overpower the cheese. Small rounds of French bread or Bremer wafers are neutral, practical choices. Any type of acidic fruit cleanses the palate. Grapes and apple slices are popular cheese complements, as are fig jam, olives, nuts, and chutney.

WINE AND CHEESE

Because cheese is the star of your show, you want wine to play a supporting role. Save the expensive port wine for another occasion. Serve complementary flavors: a hearty cheese with a hearty wine, a delicate cheese with a delicate wine. Salty cheese, such as Stilton or blue, is best counterbalanced by a sweet dessert wine such as Sauternes.

Move from light to heavy fare. You might begin with a sparkling wine and chèvre, followed by Gewürztraminer and a washed-rind cheese, then a powerful red with an aged cheese such as Asiago. In general, it's easier to pair white wine with cheese than it is red wine because the whites' lack of tannins makes them less astringent. But a bold cabernet sauvignon, merlot, or Syrah can be a perfect complement to a creamy cheese that's high in fat and protein because butterfat softens the tannins. Here are some general rules for pairing wine and cheese:

❖ Light cheeses with light wines

❖ High-acid fresh cheese with high-acid white wine

❖ Low-acid aged cheese with low-acid white wine

❖ Strong cheese with strong wine

❖ Salty cheese with dessert wine

BEER AND CHEESE

Though a beer-and-cheese combo may strike you as a cholesterol catastrophe, it's still a pub favorite in many parts of the world. The rules for pairing beer and cheese parallel those for matching wine and cheese. Light-bodied beers go well with more delicate cheeses; dark beers, ales, and stouts go well with stronger aged cheeses. In general, create the following matches:

❧ Fresh cheese with mellow beers, such as lagers and American wheat beers

❧ Soft-ripened cow's milk cheese such as Brie and Camembert with pilsners, porters, and pale ales

❧ Washed-rind cheese such as Muenster with English brown, amber, and Belgian pale ales

❧ Semi-hard cheese such as Cheddar, Edam, Gouda, Emmentaler, and Gruyère with heavier beers and ales

❧ Parmesan, Romano, and blue-veined cheese with strong partners such as stout or porter

❧ Goat cheese with India pale ales, brown ales, and porters

NONALCOHOLIC DRINKS AND CHEESE

The combination of apple cider and soft-ripened cheese is a staple of the Normandy diet we can happily borrow. Avoid sodas and other sugary drinks, but favor carbonated water—an excellent palate cleanser. The acid in fruit juice tends to kill cheese flavors, but unsweetened grape juice often enhances them in the same way wine does.

MORE IDEAS

The Artisanal Cheese Clock is a template you can use to prepare a cheese platter (www. artisanalcheese.com/cheeseclock). A creation of the Manhattan-based Artisanal Premium Cheese company, this visual aid helps you select and arrange cheeses from mild to bold. The Wisconsin Cheese Board has even more resources for party planning at www.eatwisconsincheese. com/pairings/default.aspx. You can download and print its twenty-page cheese-pairing guide, "Heightened Taste."

CHEESE DIARY

Cheese type . . . . Date made . . . .

Type of milk . . . . Quantity of milk . . . .

ADDING STARTER

❖ Culture/acid name and amount . . . .

❖ Culture/acid adding time . . . . ❖ Milk temperature. . . . .

ADDING RENNET

❖ Rennet name and amount . . . .

❖ Rennet adding time . . . . ❖ Milk temperature. . . . .

CUTTING THE CURD

❖ Size of curds . . . . ❖ Time when curds are cut. . . . .

COOKING THE CURD

❖ Time when curds are cooked . . . .

❖ Start temperature. . . . . ❖ End temperature . . . .

DRAINING THE CURD

❖ Time of draining . . . .

MILLING THE CURD

❖ Time of milling . . . .

SALTING THE CURD

❖ Amount of salt added . . . .

❖ Names and amounts of herbs . . . .

PRESSING THE CURD

❖ Days/Hours of pressing . . . .

❖ Amount of pressure at start . . . . ❖ Amount of pressure at end . . . .

AIR-DRYING

❖ Days/Hours of pressing . . . .

WAXING

❖ Date waxed . . . .

AGING

❖ Amount of time aged. ❖ Temperature and humidity . . . .

EATING

❖ Date of taste test . . . .

NOTES

. . . .

. . . .

Cheese type . . . .   Date made . . . .

Type of milk . . . .   Quantity of milk . . . .

ADDING STARTER

❖ Culture/acid name and amount . . . .

❖ Culture/acid adding time . . . .   ❖ Milk temperature . . . .

ADDING RENNET

❖ Rennet name and amount . . . .

❖ Rennet adding time . . . .   ❖ Milk temperature . . . .

CUTTING THE CURD

❖ Size of curds . . . .   ❖ Time when curds are cut . . . .

COOKING THE CURD

❖ Time when curds are cooked . . . .

❖ Start temperature . . . .   ❖ End temperature . . . .

DRAINING THE CURD

❖ Time of draining . . . .

MILLING THE CURD

❖ Time of milling . . . .

SALTING THE CURD

❖ Amount of salt added . . . .

❖ Names and amounts of herbs . . . .

PRESSING THE CURD

❖ Days/Hours of pressing . . . .

❖ Amount of pressure at start . . . .   ❖ Amount of pressure at end . . . .

AIR-DRYING

❖ Days/Hours of pressing . . . .

WAXING

❖ Date waxed . . . .

AGING

❖ Amount of time aged . . . .   ❖ Temperature and humidity . . . .

EATING

❖ Date of taste test . . . .

NOTES

. . . .

. . . .

GLOSSARY

acidification: A process in which the action of a starter culture precipitates milk protein into a semi-solid curd.

acidity: Sourness in milk.

affineur: A cheese "finisher" responsible for aging cheese.

aging: A step in cheese making in which cheese is stored at a certain temperature and relative humidity so it can ripen. Also called *curing*.

air-drying: A step in cheese making in which the pressed cheese is allowed to dry at room temperature prior to aging.

Alpine cheese: Cheese made from milk animals that grazed on Alpine grasses.

annatto: An extract from seeds of *Bixa orellana* used to give cheeses such as Cheddar an orange-yellow color.

***appellation d'origine contrôlée* (AOC):** "Term of controlled origin" is the French certification granted to certain cheeses, wines, and other agricultural products. Roquefort was the first awarded AOC status (in 1925); as of 2009, forty-four French cheeses were AOC certified.

artificial growth hormone: See *RBGH*.

artisan cheese: A cheese produced primarily by hand, in small batches, with particular attention paid to the tradition of the cheese maker's art.

ash: A food-grade charcoal sprinkled on cheeses such as Selles-sur-Cher.

bacteria: Microscopic single-cell organisms found everywhere and essential for making hard cheeses.

bandaging: The trick of wrapping a cheese in muslin and vegetable shortening to seal in moisture and protect the inside of the cheese as it ages.

beta-carotene: A pigment that acts as an antioxidant and is converted by the body to vitamin A.

bloomy-rind: A type of soft-ripened cheese in which *Penicillium candidum* is added to produce white surface mold.

blue cheese: Cheese that develops blue-green veins due to the introduction of *Penicillium roqueforti*.

Brevibacterium linens: Red bacterium used to produce pungent aroma and sharp flavor in washed-rind cheese such as Muenster and Taleggio.

brine bath: A solution of salt and water. Cheese is washed in brine to promote surface ripening or immersed in brine to salt the cheese.

butter muslin: Cotton cloth with a very tight weave used to drain cheese.

butterfat: The fat portion (cream) in milk.

calcium chloride: A drying agent added directly to milk to increase cheese yield.

California Mastitis Test (CMT): A kit that can detect high levels of somatic cells, which may mean a mastitis infection (see *mastitis*).

casein: The main protein in milk that, with the action of rennet's enzyme, coagulates to form curd.

cheddaring: A technique in which slabs of curd are stacked and turned to release whey and lower pH, causing the curd to become more acidic and rubbery.

cheese board: A hardwood board used to drain soft cheese.

cheese cave: Any environment where temperature and humidity can be controlled to promote proper maturation.

cheese cloth: Cotton cloth used for banding cheeses like Cheddar and lining molds. Most commercial cheese cloth is too loosely woven to drain soft cheese.

cheese salt: Noniodized salt.

cheese trier: A device used to test a cheese's maturity, to "try" the cheese.

cheese wrap: A permeable cellophane for wrapping cheese.

chymosin: A coagulating enzyme, found in rennet, that acts on milk casein.

clabber: To sour milk and cause it to thicken and curdle.

clean break: A test to determine whether the curd is ready to be cut. If ready, the curd will separate firmly when a knife is inserted at a 45-degree angle.

coagulation: A process by which milk congeals into a gelatinous mass.

colostrum: Milk produced during the first week of an animal's lactation.

cooking: Heating the cut curd so that it shrinks in size and expels whey.

cooperative: A member-owned and operated dairy.

cream: The fat content of milk.

creamline milk: Unhomogenized milk with a "line" that separates cream (top) from milk (bottom).

culture: A blend of lactic bacteria added to milk to acidify it and flavor cheese.

curd: The semi-solid portion of coagulated milk.

curdling: The separation of milk into liquid and solids.

curing: See *aging*.

cutting the curd: A step in cheese making in which curd is cut, vertically and horizontally, in a grid pattern to encourage whey drainage.

denominazione di origine controllata: An Italian quality assurance label for agricultural products, based on the French AOC.

direct-set culture: A lab-produced, freeze-dried powder used to start the process of acidification. Used instead of a mother culture.

draining: A step in cheese making in which curd is separated from whey by placing it in a cloth-lined colander.

enzymes: Proteins that cause biochemical changes, such as coagulation.

farmstead cheese: Cheese made with milk from the farmer's own herd, or flock, on the farm where the animals are raised.

fermentation: Curdling of milk by the action of lactic-acid-producing bacteria.

follower: The lid for a mold (container).

Geotrichum candidum: White mold used with other molds to develop flavor in soft-ripened cheese.

hard cheese: Low-moisture cheese that has been salted, pressed, and aged in a cheese cave.

heat treatment: Also called thermization. A low-temperature (145 degrees Fahrenheit) and short-time (15 seconds) method of pasteurizing milk that has the least impact on natural bacteria and enzymes.

high temperature short time (HTST): The most common method of pasteurization in which milk is held at 161 degrees Fahrenheit for at least 15 seconds.

homogenization: A process whereby milk is forced through small nozzles under great pressure. Fat globules are then so fine that they remain suspended in the milk.

hooping: Filling a mold with curd that will be pressed.

hygrometer: A device for measuring relative humidity.

inoculation: A step in cheese making in which bacteria and mold are added to milk.

lactation: A process in which milk is secreted by the mammary glands.

lactic acid: Acid produced when milk sours. In cheese making, starter-culture bacteria consume lactose and create lactic acid as a by-product.

lactose intolerance: A physical intolerance and inability to process milk sugars, often confused with milk allergy.

lactose: Milk sugar.

lipase powder: An enzyme used to produce extra acid.

Low Temperature, Long Time (LTLT): Heating milk to 145 degrees Fahrenheit for 30 minutes, also called vat pasteurization.

mastitis: An inflammation of the udder of a milk-producing animal caused by bacterial infection.

matting: The knitting together of curd into a spongy mass.

mesophilic starter culture: A blend of lactic-acid-producing bacteria used to make cheese when the temperature is between 70 and 104 degrees Fahrenheit.

milk sugar: Lactose.

milling: A step in cheese making in which curd is broken into smaller pieces before being pressed.

molds, for curd: Containers that help shape the cheese and aid in drainage. Some molds define the type of cheese.

mother culture: A homegrown, as opposed

to a commercial, starter.

natural rind: A cheese that is ripened without the protective coating of wax or cloth bandages.

nonfat milk: Milk that has a butterfat content of 1 to 2 percent.

open-vat cheese making: An artisanal process in which the cheesemaker works over an open vat.

pasta filata **cheese:** An Italian cheese that is heated until it becomes elastic and can be stretched or "spun."

paste: The inside of a cheese.

pasteurization: Heat treatment of milk to destroy pathogens. The most common method is called HTST or High Temperature, Short Time. Milk is held at 161 degrees Fahrenheit for at least 15 seconds.

Penicillium candidum: White mold that grows on the surface of soft-ripened cheese such as Brie and causes enzymatic changes in the paste.

Penicillium roqueforti: Blue mold that produces blue-green veins, sharp taste, and creamy consistency in cheeses such as Stilton and Gorgonzola.

pH meter: A device used to measure acidity.

pH scale: A device used to measure the concentration of hydrogen ions in milk—its acidity or alkalinity.

pressing: The application of pressure to remove whey and produce a drier, firmer cheese.

propionic bacteria: Used in Swiss-style cheese making to create "eyes" (holes) and a distinctive flavor.

raw milk: Unpasteurized milk—in other words, straight from the animal.

RBGH (also RBST and RBSG): Artificial growth hormones approved by the FDA for use in commercial dairies.

redressing: The process of removing a cheese from the press and its mold to turn it before further pressing.

rennet: A coagulating enzyme used to curdle milk.

Rhizomucor miehei: A mold that contains an enzyme used to make vegetable rennet.

rind: The firm surface of a pressed cheese.

ripening: The process of aging cheese for flavor development.

salting: A step in cheese making in which noniodized salt is added to curd before molding or to the surface of the pressed cheese.

set: To allow the milk to gel after adding a coagulant.

skim milk: Milk that has a butterfat content of 1 to 2 percent.

soft-ripened cheese: Unpressed high-moisture cheeses that are aged for relatively short periods, such as Camembert and Brie.

soft unripened cheese: Unpressed high-moisture cheeses that are not aged. Also called *fresh* or *bag* cheeses.

starter culture: Active lactic-acid-producing bacteria that "start" the process of cheese making.

syneresis: A process in which cut curd shrinks as it loses liquid.

terroir: French term meaning "a sense of place"; the cheese's connection to the land.

texture test: A test to check whether curd is ready for draining done by gripping a small handful. If the curd sticks together and easily crumbles apart, it is ready.

thermization: See *heat treatment.*

thermophilic starter culture: A blend of lactic-acid-producing bacteria used to make cheese when the temperature is between 86 to 132 degrees Fahrenheit.

titrated acidity: A test in which phenolphthalein is added to milk to determine its acidity or alkalinity.

tomme mold: A mold 4 inches high and 8 inches wide with a lid. It will make a 2- to 5-pound cheese.

top-stir: To stir the surface of unhomogenized milk to keep the cream from rising after rennet is added.

ultra heat-treated (UHT): Milk that has been heated to 275 to 300 degrees Fahrenheit, is often sold in cartons, and doesn't need refrigeration.

ultra-pasteurization (UP): Processing milk at a temperature from 191 to 212 degrees Fahrenheit for varying times to extend shelf life.

vat pasteurization: See Low Temperature, Long Time (LTLT).

washed-curd cheese: Cheese that has been cooked by replacing a certain amount of whey with hot water.

washed-rind cheese: A type of cheese that is regularly wiped with a solution of brine or alcohol to encourage bacterial growth.

water bath: A process in which the cheese pot is immersed in hot water, in either another larger pot or in the sink. Also called *indirect heating.*

waxing: A trick used to prevent excess drying and to retard mold on an aging cheese.

whey: The liquid portion of the milk left when milk is curdled. High in protein and carbohydrates.

whole milk: Milk that retains its original ingredients and a butterfat content of 3.5 to 4 percent.

Cheese-Making Suppliers

You can order your ingredients (except milk), equipment, and accessories from these suppliers by phone or internet.

CAPRINE SUPPLY

800-646-7736

www.caprinesupply.com

If goats are your passion, this store has what you need.

DAIRY CONNECTION, INC.

608-242-9030

www.dairyconnection.com

Sells EZAL cultures from France among other supplies and equipment.

GLENGARRY CHEESE MAKING & DAIRY SUPPLY

888-816-0903

http://glengarrycheese making.on.ca

Sells a variety of cheese-making supplies and equipment.

THE GRAPE AND GRANARY

800-695-9870

www.thegrape.net

Scroll down to find a link to their cheese-making page, which offers a range of supplies, equipment, and books on the subject.

HOEGGER SUPPLY COMPANY

800-221-4628

http://hoeggergoatsupply.com/xcart/cheese-making

Sells an excellent cheese press and other cheese-making essentials. Just click "shop."

LEENERS

800-543-3697

www.leeners.com/cheese.html

A one-stop mail-order shop for cheese makers—and with very reasonable prices.

NEW ENGLAND CHEESE MAKING SUPPLY COMPANY

413-397-2012

www.cheesemaking.com

Not only does this site sell supplies but it also acts as an international community for cheese-making instruction and discussion.

Useful Websites

THE AMERICAN CHEESE SOCIETY

www.cheesesociety.org

The American Cheese Society is the trade association for cheese makers. Their site includes membership information, regional guilds, and a definition of cheese terms and types.

CHEESE ENTHUSIAST

www.cheeseenthusiast.net
This lively newsletter covers all things artisan-cheese related.

CHEESE.COM

www.cheese.com
Explore this site to learn about different kinds of cheeses from around the world. You can search the database of 652 cheeses by name, country of origin, kind of milk that is used to produce it, or texture.

FANKHAUSER'S CHEESE PAGE

http://biology.clc.uc.edu/Fankhauser/cheese/cheese.html
David B. Fankhauser's website is chockful of cheese-making instruction and photos.

FIASCO FARM

http://fiascofarm.com
This site includes information on dairy goats and cheese making, including recipes and instructions for making a cheese press.

I LOVE CHEESE

www.ilovecheese.com
Visit ilovecheese.com to find everything cheesy, from recipes and pairings to entertaining tips. Sign up for their "Cheese Chatter" quarterly e-newsletter.

JACK SCHMIDLING PRODUCTIONS, INC.

http://schmidling.com/press.htm
This is a great source for instructions for making various cheese presses.

RAW MILK FACTS

http://raw-milk-facts.com
This is the informative website of Randolph Jonsson, a nutrition consultant in California.

SMALLDAIRY.COM

www.smalldairy.com
This site compiles links to helpful information for small commercial dairies, homesteaders, and people who want to make artisan cheese in their own kitchens.

THE CHEESEMAKER

www.thecheesemaker.com
Steve Shapson offers supplies, classes, and moral support for making Camembert and Brie. He's a great resource for beginners.

WESTON A. PRICE FOUNDATION

www.realmilk.com/why.html
This site lists sources of raw milk in states where it's legal to buy it.

Books

Amrien-Boyes, Debra, *200 Easy Homemade Cheese Recipes*, Robert Rose, 2009.

Battistotti, Bruno et al., *Cheese: A Guide to the World of Cheese and Cheese Making*, NY: Facts On File, 1984.

Carroll, Ricki, *Home Cheese Making*, 3rd Ed., Storey Publishing, 2002.

Fletcher, Janet, *Cheese and Wine: A Guide to Selecting, Pairing, and Enjoying*, NY: Chronicle Books, 2007.

_____, *The Cheese Course*; NY: Chronicle Books, 2000.

Harbutt, Juliette and Roz Denny, *The World Encyclopedia of Cheese*, London: Hermes House, 2003.

Jenkins, Steven, *The Cheese Primer*, NY: Workman Publishing, 1996.

Kindstedt, Paul, *American Farmstead Cheese*, VT: Chelsea Green, 2005.

Kosikowski, Frank and Vikram Mistry, *Cheese and Fermented Milk Foods*, 3rd Ed., vols 1 and 2. Westport: 1997.

Lambert, Paula, *The Cheese Lover's Cookbook and Guide*, NY: Simon & Schuster, 2000.

Le Jaouen, Jean-Claude, *The Fabrication of Farmstead Goat Cheese*, Cheesemaker's Journal, Ashfield, MA: 1990.

Masui, Kazuko, *French Cheeses*, NY: DK Publishing, 1996.

McCalman, Max and David Gibbons, *The Cheese Plate*, NY: Clarkson Potter, 2002.

McGee, Harold, *On Food and Cooking*, NY: Scribner, 1984.

Morris, Margaret, *The Cheesemaker's Manual*, Ontario: Glengarry Cheesemaking & Dairy Supply, 2003.

Rance, Patrick, *Cheeses of the World*, NY: Rizzoli., 2002.

Scott, R., R.K. Robinson, and R.A. Wilbey, *Cheesemaking Practice*, 3rd Ed., Gaithersburg, MD: Aspen, 1998.

Stamm, Eunice, *The History of Cheesemaking in New York State*, Published by the author, 1991.

Teubner, Christian, *The Cheese Bible*, NY: Chartwell Books, 1998.

Thorpe, Liz, *The Cheese Chronicles*, NY: Harper Collins, 2009.

Werlin, Laura, *The New American Cheese*, NY: Stewart, Tabori and Chang, 2000.

INDEX

*Page numbers or ranges in **bold** indicate a recipe for making cheese.*

PHOTO CREDITS

page 1: crolique/SS **page 6**: courtesy of Rogue Creamery **page 7**: courtesy of Cowgirl Creamery **page 8**: courtesy of Cowgirl Creamery **page 9**: courtesy of Redwood Hill Creamery **page 9**: courtesy of Cowgirl Creamery **page 10**: courtesy of The Mozzarella Company **page 11**: St. Nick/SS **page 12**: Budotradan (Wiki-CC License) **page 13**: courtesy of Cowgirl Creamery **page 14**: crolique/SS **page 15**: courtesy of Vermont Butter and Cheese Creamery **page 17**: Dave McAleavy/SS **page 18**: Tan Wei Ming/SS **page 19**: Tan Wei Ming/SS **page 20**: Elena Elisseeva/SS **page 21**: (top) RedTC/SS (bottom) WilleeCole/SS **page 23**: Lilyana Vynogradova/SS **page 25**: Shebeko/SS **page 27**: (top) F8.IN.TH/SS (bottom) Anna Kogut/SS **page 28**: Pichugin Dmitry/SS **page 29**: Ron Hilton/SS **page 30**: Simon Krzic/SS

page 31: pick/SS **page 32**: 1000 Words/SS **page 33**: Alexander Chaikin/SS **page 35**: Indigo Fish/SS **page 36**: Jean Fogle **page 37**: grongar/Flickr **page 40**: Jean Fogle **page 41**: (top) Jean Fogle (both bottom) grongar/Flickr **page 42**: (top) grongar/Flickr (bottom) Jean Fogle **page 43**: (top) Jean Fogle (both bottom) grongar/Flickr **page 44**: Jean Fogle **page 45**: (all) grongar/Flickr **page 46**: (top) grongar/Flickr (bottom) Jean Fogle **page 47**: Jean Fogle **page 48**: grongar/Flickr **page 49**: Natalia Klenova/SS **page 51**: Jovan Nikolic/SS **page 52**: (top two and bottom) grongar/Flickr (third down) Jean Fogle **page 53**: (all) grongar/Flickr **page 54**: (both) grongar/Flickr **page 55**: Jean Fogle **page 57**: Natalia Klenova/SS **page 58**: (both) Jean Fogle **page 59**: highviews/SS **page 59**: Dream79/SS **page 60**: Monkey Business Images/SS **page 61**: bonchan /SS **page 62**: Kitaeva Tatiana /SS **page 63**: Cody and Maureen/Flickr **page 64**: kiboka/SS

page 65: Digivic/SS **page 66**: Amanda Slater/Flickr **page 67**: Elke Dennis /SS **page 69**: Cathleen A Clapper/SS **page 70**: (top) margouillat photo/SS (bottom) Daniel Gilbey Photography/SS **page 71**: HLPhoto/SS **page 72**: Carmen Steiner/SS **page 73**: HLPhoto/SS

page 74: R.Ashrafov/SS **page 75**: kavring/SS **page 77**: Kati Molin/SS **page 78**: grongar/Flickr **page 80**: Jean Fogle **page 81**: marco mayer/SS **page 82**: monticello **page 83**: fotogiunta/SS

page 85: Javier Lastras/Flickr **page 86**: fotogiunta/SS **page 89**: Jean Fogle **page 90**: (top) Jean Fogle (bottom) grongar/Flickr

page 91: Josh Resnick/SS **page 92**: Yanik Chauvin/SS **page 93**: grongar/Flickr

page 95: Marie C Fields/SS **page 96**: Mark Stout Photography/SS **page 97**: Foodpictures/SS **page 98**: Ingrid Balabanova/SS **page 99**: Erik E. Cardona/SS **page 100**: Madlen/SS **page 101**: keko64/SS **page 102**: John Sullivan (Wiki-Public Domain) **page 103**: John Sullivan (Wiki-Public Domain) **page 104**: Flavio Massari/SS **page 105**: silver-john/SS **page 107**: Gayvoronskaya_yana/SS **page 108**: Denis Tabler/SS **page 109**: Petr Malyshev/SS **page 110**: lsantilli SS **page 111**: john330/SS **page 112**: Shawn Hempel/SS **page 113**: AGphotographer/SS **page 114**: Edwtie (Wiki-CC License) **page 115**: Lilyana Vynogradova/SS **page 117**: Natalia Klenova/SS **page 118**: (both) grongar/Flickr **page 119**: Andrea Skjold/SS **page 121**: msheldrake/SS

page 122: Natalia Klenova/SS **page 123**: margouillat photo/SS **page 125**: elena moiseeva/SS **page 126**: effe45/SS **page 127**: Peter Kim/SS **page 129**: Viktor1/SS **page 130**: viki2win/SS

page 131: matin/SS **page 133**: (top) Denis Tabler/SS (bottom) Jiri Hera/SS **page 135**: Natalia Klenova/SS **page 136**: Grongar/Flickr **page 137**: Nailia Schwarz/SS **page 139**: shyshak roman/SS **page 140**: Christopher Elwell/SS **page 142**: Lilyana Vynogradova/SS **page 143**: Véronique PAGNIER (Wiki-CC License) **page 144**: Fedor Kondratenko/SS **page 145**: Jean Fogle **page 149**: Baloncici **page 150**: effe45 **page 153**: Dream79/SS

page 154: Gustavo Toledo/SS **page 156**: margouillat photo/SS **page 157**: Pvt pauline (Wiki-CC License) **page 159**: msheldrake/SS **page 161**: Brenda Carson/SS **page 162**: Feraru Nicolae/SS **page 163**: (top) Monkey Business Images/SS (bottom) Jean Fogle **page 164**: crolique/SS **page 165**: Jean Fogle

/SS = Shutterstock.com
/Flickr = from Flickr under the Creative Commons License

Cole Dawson

Journalist Lisa Mullenneaux, writing here under the pen name Cole Dawson, lives in New York's Hudson Valley, an area rich in farmstead cheese making. Her ancestors in Orange County practiced fruit farming and would, she hopes, approve of today's buy-local food movement. The author began her career at *Westways* magazine in Los Angeles, working with major authors, photographers, and artists on the West Coast. Returning to New York State in 1990, she edited law books at Matthew Bender Co. while contributing to magazines and newspapers on travel, health, and food. She is the New York City correspondent for the global news syndicate www.relaxnews.com. Her three previous books include *Sleep Cheap in New York: High-Quality Lodgings at Rock-Bottom Rates*, *Ni una Bomba Más: Vieques vs. U.S. Navy*, and *Vermont Antiquing: Seven Day Trips*.